MORE Things You Can Do To Defend Your Gun Rights

Other Books by the Authors

By Alan M. Gottlieb and David B. Kopel

Things You Can Do to Defend Your Gun Rights

by Alan M Gottlieb

The Rights of Gun Owners

The Gun Grabbers

Gun Rights Fact Book

Alan Gottlieb's Celebrity Address Book

With George Flynn:

Guns For Women

With Ron Arnold:

Trashing the Economy

By David B. Kopel

The Samurai, the Mountie, the Cowboy: Should America Adopt the Gun Controls of Other Democracies?

Gun Control in Great Britain: Saving Lives or Constricting Liberty?

Guns: Who Should Have Them?

MORE
Things
You Can Do
To Defend
Your
Gun Rights

By

Alan Gottlieb

and

Dave Kopel

MERRIL PRESS
BELLEVUE, WASHINGTON

MORE Things You Can Do To Defend Your Gun Rights
COPYRIGHT © 1995
BY ALAN M. GOTTLIEB AND DAVID B. KOPEL

For information, permissions, or additional copies of this book, contact Merril Press, PO Box 1682, Bellevue, Washington 98009. Telephone (206) 454-7009.

$9.95   ISBN: 0-936783-13-3

Printed in the United States of America

Table of Contents

Dedication

To our children, Amy, Merril, Alexis, and Andrew
and Katie, Maggie, and Andrew
who we hope will live in a freer, more tolerant society.

User's Warning
This book attempts to provide information about methods to preserve and protect the rights we all share. Some of the advice is based on first-hand experience, and some is based on recommendations of others. While we've tried to make the book as accurate as possible, we can't promise or guarantee particular results. It is the reader's responsibility to put the book to use in an appropriate manner.

A Note on Usage
Half the people in country are female, so we thought it inappropriate to use "he" and "him" exclusively. At the same time, we thought it cumbersome to always say "he or she." So some of the time we use "he" by itself, and sometimes we use "she" by itself. The gender pronoun chosen never has any significance, and everything in this book applies equally to men and women.

Introduction

In September 1993, as the Second Amendment stood on the brink of disaster, our book, *Things You Can Do to Protect Your Gun Rights* was published. The gun rights movement, having fought a defensive, holding action in Washington since 1988, was under the greatest attack in history. Within a few months, the Brady Bill passed. As we expected, the passage of this "reasonable" law did not lead the anti-gun movement to moderate its demands; to the contrary, the anti-rights movement rolled out an even more ambitious agenda for choking the Second Amendment, and the media plunged into the greatest anti-gun feeding frenzy in American history.

A ban on over 200 semi-automatic firearms passed the U.S. Senate by one vote in November 1993, and passed the House by a similar margin in May 1994—after House Speaker Tom Foley used an unlawful "long count" to give the gun banners time to apply pressure and turn a narrow defeat into a narrow victory for gun prohibition.

The gun prohibition lobbies and their allies in the White House and Congress were jubilant. They were certain that the Brady Bill and the ban on over 200 guns were just the beginning of the rapid eradication of what remained of the Second Amendment.

But the gun banners were radically wrong. All over the United States, friends of freedom got to work. Many of them used the tactics we detailed in *Things You Can Do to Protect Your Gun Rights*. As a result, the infamous Clinton crime bill and its gun ban were blocked and very nearly defeated. Only the furious lobbying and bribing of a desperate President finally saved the anti-Constitutional crime bill.

It would prove to be a Pyhrric victory for the gun banners, the President, and their Congressional allies. Forcing the criminal "crime bill" through Congress cost Clinton and his allies in the House and Senate (mis)leadership their last remnants of political capital, thereby ensuring the that Clinton scheme for the federal government to take over and ration all health care in the country would never pass.

On November 8, 1994, grassroots, pro-rights activists all over the United States fired the anti-Constitutional Congress people who had done the bidding of the gun ban lobbies. From Tom Andrews in Maine to Tom Foley in Washington, from Harris Wofford in Pennsylvania to Buddy Darden in Georgia, many anti-gun Congressmen suddenly found that they were *ex*-Congress-men. From obscure state legislators to the mighty Speaker of the House, politician after politician was removed from office through the dedicated grassroots work of pro-rights citizen activists. We won one of the greatest victories in the history of American politics.

And today, gun rights activists are not going to go back to sleep. They know that the new crop of legislators in Congress will need constant feedback from the home folks in order to counteract the corrosive, big-government influence of Washington.

They know that rolling back all of the advances of the anti-Constitution lobbies will take years of work, including work in the 1996 and 1998 election. Enacting new pro-freedom legislation will not come easily.

Today's activists know that the anti-gun groups will be working as hard as ever to undermine the Second Amendment, and that no victories or defeats in politics are ever permanent.

So to those activists who understand, as did abolitionist leader Wendell Phillips, that "eternal vigilance is the price of liberty," we present this new book. While our first book focused on direct political action—such as writing letters to legislators, or participating in political campaigns—most of this new book deals with longer term projects: how to use your money so that it supports the friends (rather than the enemies) of freedom; how gun clubs, gun stores, and gun companies can do their share; how to educate the next generation about the importance of the Second Amendment.

In the final section of the book, we conclude not with specific tips for action, but with advice about how activists can best approach the gun issue: how to recognize the high stakes involved in our battle for freedom, and how to fight our wars with vigor, with determination, and with compassion.

As with our first book, we hope that this book proves useful not just to Second Amendment activists, but to anyone who is fighting the good fight for freedom, humankind's oldest and noblest cause.

PART I

SOCIALLY RESPONSIBLE
USE OF YOUR MONEY

Money talks. In fact, it screams. This section looks at how you can make sure your money works for your ideals. There's a lot more you can do with your money in addition to donating it to pro-rights organizations. Much more of your dollars can be invested and spent in ways that will help the Second Amendment—and often save you money in the bargain.

1. Defund the Opposition

"THE STRENGTH OF THE CONSTITUTION LIES ENTIRELY IN THE DETERMI-
NATION OF EACH CITIZEN TO DEFEND IT. ONLY IF EVERY SINGLE CITIZEN
FEELS DUTY BOUND TO DO HIS SHARE IN THIS DEFENSE ARE CONSTITU-
TIONAL RIGHTS SECURE."
—Albert Einstein.

Who are the anti-gun movement? In terms of actual members, the two largest anti-gun lobbies are pretty small. Handgun
Control, Inc. has about a quarter million members. (Yet their advertising claims they are "two million strong.") The Coalition to
Stop Gun Violence is even smaller. So how do these small groups
create the impression that they speak for large numbers of the
American people?

One of their strategies is to win endorsements from other
organizations. And since the endorsing organizations represent a
lot of people, the impression is built that a lot of people strongly
believe in gun control. Few of these organizations, however, ask
their membership what the membership thinks. But in Washington, it is generally assumed (wrongly) that leaders of organizations represent the views of their members.

What do these various endorsing groups have in common?
One way or another, almost all of them have some ideological or
financial interest in expanded government and diminished personal
liberty. Some of the organizations are made up of government
employees (especially employees of government schools); others,
many of the medical groups for example, receive a significant share
of their income through government programs (such as Medicare
and Medicaid). Still other groups, such as the League of Women
Voters, simply support big government because they believe in it.

The list below was compiled from the advertisements of
the anti-gun groups. Most organizations listed below earned a
place on the list by being 1. A supporter of the Brady Bill ("Brady");
2. A supporter of Senator John Chafee's proposal to confiscate

all handguns ("Chafee"); 3. a member of the Coalition to Stop Gun Violence ("Coalition"), which supports the confiscation of handguns and semiautomatics, and stringent regulation of all other guns; or 4. a signer of a Handgun Control, Inc. advertisement demanding a nationwide assault on the Constitution through a ban on semi-automatics ("assault").

It's interesting to observe how many supporters of the "moderate" Brady Bill (requiring government permission to own a handgun) also support confiscation of handguns. The Brady Bill could have been stopped, if more gun owners had recognized that the bill was simply an opening wedge for much more radical schemes.

But it's also important to note that only one of the police groups which supported the Brady Bill also supports handgun confiscation.

And now, a who's who of the anti-gun movement's allies:

Political/Lobbying/Government Organizations

American Association of Retired Persons (AARP). This group vociferously supports gun control laws, based on a false claim to have polled the membership on the gun issue. If you're a present or former AARP member, when you write to elected officials, make sure to let them know that the AARP does not speak for you on gun control.

Larry Pratt, the head of Gun Owners of America, has written an excellent exposé of how AARP rips off its members through overpriced insurance, and then rips them off more by lobbying for big government programs that the members may not support. Copies of Pratt's report on AARP can be obtained by sending five dollars to Gun Owners of America, 8001 Forbes Place, Suite 102, Springfield, VA 22151.

Happily, a new organization, the Seniors Coalition, has been formed to lobby for the genuine interests of senior citizens. Unlike the AARP, the Seniors Coalition did not support the Clinton plan to socialize, ration, and ruin American health care. Unlike

AARP, the Seniors Coalition does not fight against the Balanced Budget Amendment. Unlike the AARP, the Seniors Coalition is totally independent, and does not accept money from the federal government. The Coalition's Director of Government Affairs is Jake Hansen, formerly a pro-gun Senator from Utah. So if you're fifty or older, stop wasting money on the AARP, and consider joining the Senior Coalition. (703) 591-0663.

Americans for Democratic Action (Brady, Coalition, Assault). An organization of political liberals that was on the cutting edge when it was founded in the 1940s by folks like Arthur Schlesinger, Jr. and Reinhold Neibuhr. Now, a mostly irrelevant repository of paleo-liberalism, with no ideas of post-1966 vintage.

Center for Science in the Public Interest (Coalition, Chafee). A misnamed, anti-scientific group of Luddites, dedicated to outlawing as many new technologies as possible.

Child Welfare League (Coalition).

Children's Defense Fund (Chafee, Brady). This one is run by Hillary Clinton's very good friend Marion Wright Edelman. Mrs. Clinton has served as Chair of the Fund's board of directors. Despite the use of "Children" in the name, the group is and always has been primarily dedicated to fighting welfare reform. The group is increasingly active in producing anti-gun propaganda.

National Association for the Advancement of Colored People (Brady). Formerly one of the greatest civil rights organizations in human history, the NAACP under its present leadership is a loud supporter of gun prohibition, and an increasingly shrill advocate for all forms of political correctness and racial quotas. The NAACP Legal Defense Fund, which in better days helped bring forth some of the most important Constitutional rights cases in American history, is now on the anti-Constitutional side, as a supporter of product liability suits against gun manufacturers.

National Association of Counties (Brady, Assault). Hardly any counties ever chose to ban "assault weapons" or to impose waiting periods, yet the national association hypocritically told Congress to do what the counties had chosen not to do.

National Coalition Against Domestic Violence (Chafee).

National League of Cities (Brady, Assault).

National Organization for Women (Brady) is a group dedicated to the belief that the best path to liberation for women is found through allowing the federal government to attain increased power. NOW leaders appear frequently in women's magazines to criticize the idea that women should use guns to resist rapists and other male criminals.

National Rainbow Coalition (Brady). The organization of Jesse Jackson, a supporter of handgun confiscation.

National Urban Coalition (Brady).

National Urban League (Coalition, Brady).

Public Citizen's Congress Watch (Assault). Ralph Nader's group.

U.S. Conference of Mayors (Coalition, Brady, Chafee, Assault).

U.S. Student Association (Coalition).

Women's National Democratic Club (Coalition, Assault).

Women's National Democratic Club (Assault).

Professional Associations or Unions

American Association of School Administrators (Chafee).

American Federation of State, County, and Municipal Employees (Brady, Assault).

Brotherhood of Maintenance Way Employees (Brady).

Council of Great City Schools (Chafee).

Food and Allied Service Trades, AFL-CIO (Brady).

Hotel Employees & Restaurant Employees International Union, AFL-CIO (Brady).

International Ladies Garment Workers Union (Brady, Assault).

National Association of Community Health Centers (Chafee).

National Association of Convenience Stores (Brady).

National Association of School Psychologists (Chafee).

National Association of Social Workers (Coalition, Brady,

Chafee, Assault). The organization which helped inflict one of the greatest disasters ever caused by excessive government (the poverty-causing "welfare" system) is hard at work to get us even more big government disasters.

National Education Association (NEA). Supporters of all kinds of gun control, and vehement opponents of all measures to give students and parents greater choice in education. One of the most powerful lobbies in the United States, and one of the most destructive. Although many good, dedicated teachers are among the members, the group's ideology drifts further left every year, with heavy emphasis on government reconditioning of students who do not display politically correct attitudes.

Public Employee Dept., AFL-CIO (Brady, Assault).

Medical Organizations:

American Academy of Pediatrics (Chafee, Brady, Assault). By far the most radical and pro-government of all the medical organizations. They even want to outlaw BB guns.

American Association for the Surgery of Trauma (Chafee).

American Association of Suicidology (Coalition).

American College of Emergency Physicians (Brady).

American Medical Student Association (Brady, Assault).

American Nurses Association (Brady, Assault). A 1994 House of Delegates resolution orders the ANA to support legislation restricting the sale and availability of handguns.

American Psychiatric Association (Coalition).

American Public Health Association (Coalition, Chafee, Assault).

American Trauma Society (Chafee).

Center on Addiction and Substance Abuse at Columbia University (Chafee). A research organization run by former Johnson/Carter bigwig Joseph Califano.

Conference of State and Territorial Injury Prevention Directors (Chafee).

National Association of Children's Hospitals and Related Institutions (Brady, Assault).

National Association of Orthopedic Nurses (Brady).

National Association of Pediatric Nurse Associates and Practitioners (Assault).

National Recovery Institute. This group ran an anti-drug commercial showing a revolver being loaded one bullet at a time. The message compared using drugs to loading a revolver to commit suicide. Besides promoting hysteria, the commercial insinuated that guns (which are legal) are just as supposedly despicable as drugs (which are illegal).

Physicians for Social Responsibility (Assault). These are the same geniuses who told everybody that the best prescription for the "medical" problem of the Cold War was unilateral American nuclear disarmament. With the Cold War now over (no thanks to these folks), the group now tries to convince American crime victims that the proper "medical" response to crime is for the victims to unilaterally disarm.

Police Organizations

Federal Law Enforcement Officers Association (Brady, Assault).

Fraternal Order of Police (Brady).

International Association of Chiefs of Police (Brady). The IACP has supported handgun prohibition since the early years of the 20th century; they accept police chiefs from freedom-loving nations like Iraq as members.

International Brotherhood of Police Officers (Brady).

Major City Chiefs Administrators (Brady, Assault).

National Alliance for Safe Schools (Chafee)(affiliate of a law enforcement organization).

National Association of Police Organizations (Brady, Assault).

National Organization of Black Law Enforcement Executives (Brady, Assault).

Police Executive Research Forum (Brady, Assault).

Police Foundation (Brady, Assault).

Service Organizations

General Federation of Women's Clubs (Brady, Assault).

League of Women Voters of the U.S. (Brady, Assault). Formerly a non-partisan "good-government" group dedicated to providing unbiased information about choices facing voters. Today, an advocate for big government of all types.

National Council of Negro Women (Coalition).

National Congress of Parents and Teachers (PTA) (Brady). Despite the word "parents" in the title, the group is indistinguishable from other education bureaucracy lobbies dedicated to fighting school choice and parental empowerment.

YWCA of the USA (Assault).

Religious organizations:

American Baptist Churches. These folks picketed NRA headquarters weekly during the summer of 1993.

American Ethical Union (Coalition, Chafee).

American Jewish Committee (Coalition, Brady, Assault)

American Jewish Congress (Coalition, Brady, Assault).

Anti-Defamation League (Brady, Assault).

B'nai B'rith International (Brady).

B'nai B'rith Woman (Coalition).

Central Conference of American Rabbis (Coalition).

Church of the Brethren, Washington Office (Brady, Coalition, Assault).

Evangelical Lutheran Church in America. (Brady). The ELCA supports a system that "rigidly controls" handguns and "assault weapons."

Friends Committee on National Legislation (Coalition, Chafee).

Jesuit Conference, Office of Social Ministries (Coalition, Chafee).

Mennonite Central Comm., Washington Office (Brady, Assault).

National Council of Jewish Women (Coalition).

National Jewish Welfare Board (Coalition).

Presbyterian Church (USA)-The Program Agency (Chafee, Coalition).

The Bible Holiness Movement, International (Coalition).

Union of American Hebrew Congregations(Coalition, Brady).

Unitarian Universalist Association (Coalition, Chafee, Brady).

United Church of Christ-Center for Social Action (Chafee, Coalition, Assault).

United Methodist Church. (Chafee, Coalition, Brady, Assault). These folks are the principle founder of the National Coalition to Ban Handguns (which is now called the Coalition to Stop Gun Violence).

United Synagogues of America (Coalition).

Women's League for Conservative Judaism (Coalition).

Young Women's Christian Association of the USA, National Board (Coalition).

Finally, one other institution deserves a place in the anti-gun Ring of Shame. In June 1993, Drexel University awarded an honorary degree to James and Sarah Brady, certifying them as a "doctor of humane letters." If Drexel thinks that assaulting the Constitution is a "humane" thing to do, then you can probably find other institutions of higher learning which better deserve your support.

Strategy

How should you deal with these groups? If you're a member, of, for example, a Presbyterian church, make sure that you give money to church projects in your community or elsewhere, but don't give money which will flow towards the national headquarters politicos.

You can also urge that the local chapter of the organization you belong to (such as a local PTA) enact a resolution dissociating the local group from the national organization's endorsement of gun control. Once the resolution is adopted, send copies to your elected officials, to the national headquarters, and to the NRA.

And if you are not already a member, and you are sent a mail solicitation to join one of these groups, read the letter to find out how much money they want you to give them. Then send a check for the same amount to NRA (800-648-4672), the Second Amendment Foundation (206-454-7012) or another pro-rights group. You can even use the postage-paid reply envelope that the anti-gun group sent you to send them back a short (and polite!) note explaining that you will not contribute to a group that wants to take away basic American rights, and that you are sending a contribution instead to a pro-rights organization.

Won't that be a nice turnabout—transforming a mass mailing for the anti-rights alliance into a fundraising vehicle for the right to bear arms!

The Washington Mentality

Many of the anti-gun, public policy groups listed above are based on Washington, D.C. Only rarely are their memberships clamoring for them to do something about gun control. AARP doesn't support gun control because its retiree members are demanding repeal of the Constitution. Rather, AARP is headquartered in Washington, D.C., and its staff "networks" with the same crowd of Beltway insiders who don't trust the Americans outside the Beltway.

If you don't think Washington can have a corrosive effect on people's thinking, consider this story. Citizens Committee for the Right to Keep and Bear Arms (CCRKBA) lobbyist John Snyder doesn't spend a lot of time hobnobbing. But when one of his friends invited him to a party at one of the embassies, he decided to go along.

At the embassy party, he met an attractive young American woman. They chatted amiably for several minutes. Then she asked what he did. He told he was a lobbyist for the Citizens Committee to Keep and Bear Arms. She turned away in disgust, remarking, "I thought you were so nice."

2. *Tell Corporations to Leave Our Rights Alone*

"THOUGH I HAVE NO DOUBT EXCEPTIONS CAN BE BROUGHT FOR-
WARD, I THINK THE FOLLOWING RULE WOULD BE FOUND TO BE
GENERALLY TRUE: THAT IN AGES IN WHICH THE DOMINANT WEAPON
IS CHEAP AND SIMPLE, THE COMMON PEOPLE WILL HAVE A
CHANCE..."
                              —George Orwell, *Essays*, Volume IV.

You probably don't make weekly contributions to the gun
prohibition lobbies. At least not directly. But every day, millions
of gun owners inadvertently give money to companies which use
corporate profits to promote restrictions on the right to keep and
bear arms.

As a legal matter, the corporations have every right to
spend their money as they see fit. And so do you.

You shouldn't spend your hard-earned money on corporations that want to restrict your rights. Because America is such
a large, wealthy nation, there are a plenitude of consumer products companies who, instead of using their resources to shill for
gun control, use corporate resources to improve the standard of
living for the company's employees and stockholders.

The gun prohibitionists, of course, call us "bullies" when
we exercise our right not to spend money on companies that oppose Constitutional rights. Let them complain. Most Americans
agree that boycotting a company whose activities harm the country is a good idea. In a poll conducted by the market research firm
Oxtoby-Smith, 72% of consumers approved of boycotts.

So here are some of the companies that have supported
gun control one way or another. Included for some companies are
the address and telephone number. If you write a polite letter and/
or make a polite phone call to corporate headquarters, you can
help these companies realize that corporate assistance to enemies
of the Constitution is not only bad for the country, it's bad for the
bottom line.

Chesebrough-Pond's USA Corp. This massive consumer products company manufactures Faberge, Prince Matchabelli, Brut, Aviance, Close-up, Pepsodent, Vaseline products, Q-tips, Cutex, and Pond's. One Chesebrough advertising campaign named Sarah Brady an American hero for being a "Lifesaver and Crusader."

"Lifesaver"?! Tell that to the families of the 22 people murdered in the Luby's Cafeteria in Killeen, Texas, in October 1991 by a deranged criminal. Dr. Suzanna Gratia was in the cafeteria, and could have taken the murderer out with one shot since the gunman had his back turned on her. But Dr. Gratia didn't have her gun; she had left it in her car to comply with a Texas law that makes it impossible for law-abiding citizens like Dr. Gratia to obtain a permit to carry a gun for protection.

The Texas legislature had almost reformed the law a few months before, but effective lobbying by Mrs. Brady's self-defense prohibition organization (Handgun Control, Inc.), killed the bill in the House Calendars Committee. As a result of Mrs. Brady's success, both of Dr. Gratia's parents, and 20 other innocent victims, were killed.

Chesebrough-Pond's is located at 33 Benedict Place, Box 6000, Greenwich, CT 068360-5308. (203) 661-2000.

Crystal Dynamics. A video game producer with violent titles such as "Crash and Burn." CEO Strauss Zelnick told the *New York Times* that violent video games for children should not be censored. Instead, "let's do something real about gun control."

Diesel Jeans. In April 1993, the company ran print advertising which showed three handguns pointed at the reader. "Teaching kids to kill helps them deal directly with reality," the text read. "If they never learn to blast the brains out of their neighbors, what kind of future has this country got?" One of the magazines that ran the ad, *Premiere*, received more protests than for any other ad in the magazine's history; the magazine, for the first time in its history, apologized in a later issue for accepting the advertisement. Diesel Jeans acknowledged that the wording was "way too rough," and lamely explained that the copy was written by a Swedish advertising agency which didn't quite have the feel for American slang. "We meant to say we were against guns," a Diesel executive explained.

Esprit. This women's clothing manufacturer advertises heavily in women's magazines.

One series of ads asked the question "If you could change the world, what would you do?" Esprit chose to run the response of one woman: "There'd be no guns. No guns at all." As a trailer to the ad, Esprit provided the address for Handgun Control's tax-exempt arm, the Center to Prevent Handgun Violence.

Placing the ad in women's magazines such as *Vogue* and *Elle*, Esprit provided about $100,000 in free advertising to the anti-gun movement.

Esprit's pretext was that it was simply providing information, but Esprit offered no information about how to contact groups like the NRA, which work to reduce gun violence without infringing freedom.

When concerned women wrote to Esprit, the company didn't even have the courtesy to reply.

Esprit, PO Box 77098, San Francisco, CA 94107. (415) 648-5900.

Fireman's Fund. This insurance company ran advertising telling how satisfied Jim and Sarah Brady were with their Fireman's Fund policy, after their home suffered smoke damage. "Jim and Sarah Brady Definitely Have Prestige" said the ad's headline. Nothing wrong with insurance companies running ads from satisfied customers. Nothing wrong with insurance customers choosing companies that don't add to the prestige of people who want to destroy the Second Amendment. Firearm's Fund Insurance Co., 777 San Marin Drive, Novato CA 94998-0001. (415) 899-2000.

Health Net: This company is California's second largest health maintenance organization. It is also a massive funder of anti-gun propaganda through donations to the misnamed California Wellness Foundation. The Foundation is running a huge, multi-million dollar hoplophobe "public education" campaign in California.

Health Net, 21600 Oxnard St., Suite 1700, Woodland Hills, CA, 91367-4975. (818) 719-6705.

Johnson & Johnson. This huge consumer health and beauty products company is staunchly anti-gun. For example, the company distributed a "Health Profile Questionnaire" to MCI employees. The questionnaire included anti-gun propaganda: "Did you know that firearms are the second largest cause of fatal injuries in the U.S.? Having a handgun in your home or car increases your risk of accidental death or injury." Then came the actual health question: "Do you keep a handgun at home or in your motor vehicle?"

Quite obviously, the questionnaire was intended to discourage people from choosing to own firearms.

Johnson & Johnson Consumer Products, Inc., 199 Grandview Rd., Skilman, NJ 08558-9418. (908) 874-1000; (800) 526-3967.

Penthouse Magazine: The August 1989 issue of *Penthouse* contained a vicious parody of the "I'm the NRA" advertisement.

In the *Penthouse* version, then-President Bush was "quoted" praising the American "quality of death," touting the advantages of "Shooting an enemy," claiming that the Second Amendment guarantees the right to "shoot troublemakers" and bragging about having "blood on my hands" by virtue of his NRA membership.

Since *Penthouse* exists only because of an absolutist interpretation of the First Amendment, the magazine's vituperative assault on the Second Amendment is extraordinarily hypocritical.

Many people concerned about women's rights have been boycotting *Penthouse* ever since a 1985 issue included a "photo spread" featuring a naked Asian woman hanging from a tree, apparently dead. 1965 Broadway, NY, NY 10023-5904. (212) 496-6100.

In contrast to *Penthouse*, *Playboy* magazine has provided balanced coverage of the gun issue, running pro-and-con articles on guns, and conducting interviews with proponents and opponents of gun control.

RCA Records. The company held a press conference with RCA singer Al Green and Jim Brady, to promote Brady's Center to Prevent Handgun Violence. Al Green unveiled his song *Leave the Guns at Home.* And RCA began distributing "public service" anti-gun commercials.

Royal Bank of Canada: The Canadian bank aided the circulation of petitions calling for outlawing of semi-automatic firearms, petitions which eventually resulted in the Canadian government drastically restricting the ownership of all types of semiautomatics, even rimfires.

Time-Warner: For sheer hypocrisy, RCA doesn't come close to communications giant Time-Warner. One of the company's subsidiaries, DC Comics, has turned the venerable hero Batman into a lobbyist for Handgun Control.

In a *Batman* issue published in early 1993, some northern gang members drove down to Virginia to buy crime guns. Then the criminals quickly and easily converted their legally-purchased semiautomatics into machine guns.

Not by coincidence, Handgun Control was at that exact time lobbying the Virginia legislature to outlaw many semiautomatics, and to ration gun rights, so that nobody could buy more than one handgun in a month. (HCI admits, by the way, that the gun rights rationing law is unenforceable without registration of all handguns, and a ban on private handgun transfers.)

To make sure everyone got the point, DC Comics mailed 300 copies of the *Batman* issue to the Virginia legislature. And profits from the sale of the issue were donated to gun control efforts.

While Time-Warner was busy trying to stop violence by taking away the Constitutional rights of Virginians, Time-Warner was also busy releasing the infamous "Cop-Killer" song by rapper Ice-T. The song features a character with a sawed-off shotgun who goes hunting for police officers: "I got my ski mask on...I'm 'bout to bust some shots off...Die, Pig, Die! Fuck the police!" Not long after the song's release, a Nevada teenager inspired by the song attempted to murder a police officer.

When the Law Enforcement Alliance of America (800-766-8578) called on Time-Warner to pull the record, Time-Warner claimed that LEAA was attacking the First Amendment.

The claim was nonsense. The First Amendment forbids censorship by government. The First Amendment does not forbid corporations from acting in a responsible matter by not inciting murder.

But at least Time-Warner did its best to ensure that all the gang members the company inspired to murder police officers wouldn't be able to buy more than one gun per month.

Time-Warner, Inc. 75 Rockefeller Plaza, NY, NY 10019-6908. (212) 484-8000.

Tobacco lobby. Nicotine, the most addictive drug in the world, kills more people than all illegal drugs combined. One of the lowest points ever for the tobacco lobby came in May 1990, when Californians voted on a ballot initiative, Proposition 99, to raise the tobacco tax.

The lobby's response? It ran a TV ad that said that if tobacco taxes went up, street gangs would smuggle tobacco and use the money to buy guns. The television showed pictures of children on a jungle gym, and then pictures of white chalk outlining where children lay dead from gunfire. "More guns might not cause more murders, but is it worth taking the chance that even one more innocent person may be killed? Proposition 99 would create major crime."

Thus, to save protect itself from a 25 cent per pack tax increase, the tobacco lobby deliberately inflamed anti-gun hysteria in California. The tobacco lobby decided that its profits were more important than your rights.

Who created the ads? Roger Ailes. The mastermind of George Bush's dishonest 1988 advertising campaign in which Bush falsely promised to protect the right to bear arms.

If you think this sort of anti-gun smear campaign by the nicotine lobby is reprehensible, drop them a line at Tobacco Institute, 1875 Eye St. NW, Washington, D.C. 20006. (Technically, the Tobacco Institute didn't pay for the smear campaign; its members did.)

And finally, for several years, rumors have been circulating that Anheuser-Busch—brewer of Budweiser, Michelob, and Busch—is anti-gun. The rumors are entirely false. In truth, the company sponsors numerous shooting events, including the Trapshooting Association's Grand American Tournament.

So next time you down a Michelob, remember that you're nor only doing your taste buds a favor, you're supporting a company that supports responsible gun ownership.

Business Executives

The following businessmen gave individual financial contributions or other support to the California handgun ban initiative in 1982. Although these men are affiliated with major corporations, the corporations themselves did not necessarily play a role in the handgun ban battle:

David Packard and William Hewlett. Officers of Hewlett-Packard Corporation.

Armand Hammer. Chairman of the Board, Occidental Petroleum. Enjoyed a close relationship with the pre-*Glasnost* Soviet dictatorship.

Walter Gerken. Chairman of the Board, Pacific Mutual Life Insurance Co.

Justin Dart. Chairman of the Board, Dart Industries.

Otis Chandler. Publisher, *Los Angeles Times* (a major anti-gun newspaper).

In Virginia, when the anti-gun movement was ramming the "one-handgun-per-month" Constitutional rights rationing scheme through the legislature, the following executives assisted the anti-gun lobby, and even took out a public advertisement proclaiming their support for the gun restrictions:

Thomas Allen, Chairman of the Board, East Coast Oil Co.

Thomas Capps, President & CEO, Dominion Resources.

Joshua P. Darden, NationsBank Center.

William de Rusha. Heilig-Meyers Furniture Co.

John M. Franck. CEO. Tultex Corp.

William F. Fritsche, Jr. President & CEO. Virginia Natural Gas.

Bruce Gottwald, Ted Gottwald. Ethyl Corp.

Willie E. Lanier, John L. McElroy, Mr. & Mrs. James C. Wheat the Third. Wheat First Securities.

Frank G. Louthan. Retired President. Richmond Eng. Co.

Phyllis Marstiller. President. Blue Cross/Blue Shield of Virginia.

Randolph McElroy. President. NationsBank.

Mr. & Mrs. Arnold B. McKinnon. Chairman (and spouse). Norfolk & Southern Corp.

Robert Norfleet, Jr., President. Capital Region Crestar Bank.

Thomas G. Rosenthal. President. Standard Drug Co.

Mr. & Mrs. Bradford C.F. Sauer the Third. C.F. Sauer & Co.

Dwight Schar. Chairman. N.V.-Ryan Corp.

John Snow. President & CEO. CSX Corp.

Hugh R. Stallard. President & CEO. C&P Telephone Co.

Mr. & Mrs. Wallace Stettinius. Chairman (and spouse). CADMUS Communications Corp.

James Ukrop. President & CEO. Ukrop's Super Markets.

Robert C. Williams. President & CEO. James River Corp.

In addition, Hasbro Toys Chairman Alan Hassenfield is a leading member of the Rhode Island Coalition Against Gun Violence, and has appeared at Rhode Island rallies featuring James and Sarah Brady and handgun confiscation advocate Senator John Chafee. Hasbro states that he is speaking only for himself, and not on behalf of the company.

Finding the Company's Address

While we list some addresses above, there will certainly be other companies which make the mistake of helping the opponents of the Constitution. To track down corporate addresses, the best source is your public library, which should have the reference book *Directory of Corporate Affiliations*. The library may also have *The National Directory of Addresses and Phone Numbers* (published by Omnigraphics, Detroit, Mich.), which lists addresses and phones for most national businesses.

Make it Hurt

Write the company a letter, and tell them why you are not buying their products any more. Let them know that you will be suggesting to your pro-gun friends than they do the same. (And then of course do tell your pro-gun friends.) Here's a sample letter:

Mr. Joe Bigboss
President, Acme Products
666 Fifth Avenue
New York, 10089

Dear Mr. Bigboss [or "Dear Acme Products" if you don't know the name of an executive there]:

I am writing to let you know that I will no longer be buying Acme Products, such as the Veeblefetzer lawn mower. Instead, I will purchase products from your competitors, such as Good Guys, Inc.

I am boycotting your products because Acme was a sponsor of the recent NBZ program, "Ran Dather Tells Lies About Guns." The program was very inaccurate. For example, Mr. Dather claimed that "The average gun owner kills two or three people in cold blood every year."

I will also suggest to my friends who support the Constitutional right to bear arms that they stop buying your products.

You'll likely get back a slick reply letter from the company's public relations department. Don't worry. The more letters the company gets, the more worried they will be. As few as a dozen letters have convinced some companies to stop sponsoring shows.

When you switch your purchases to another company. write a letter to your new company, and tell them why you are buying their products, and avoiding their competitor. Your letter will help them resist future temptation to support the gun prohibition movement, or to sponsor anti-gun television and radio shows and advertisements.

Local Businesses

Local retail businesses which support gun prohibition should also be targeted by pro-rights consumers. To have any realistic chance of success, you need to focus your fire on retail companies or products (since they depend on consumer support). You also need to make sure that you and the group working on the boycott are ready for a great deal of work over a long period of time.

Methods of publicizing the boycott include picketing and leafleting in front of the store (do it on a Monday, and alert the media), as well as mentioning the boycott in pro-gun newsletters, and perhaps even making bumper stickers.

Be sure that the business really deserves a boycott. Giving $5,000 to a gun ban campaign probably counts; giving $5,000 to a legislator who, among many other issues, favors gun control, does not.

And do not engage in secondary boycotts. (A secondary boycott is boycotting an inoffensive store simply because it sells products from the company you are boycotting.)

3. Gifts and Passages: Passing on Freedom

"THINK OF YOUR FOREFATHERS! THINK OF YOUR POSTERITY!"
—John Quincy Adams, Speech at Plymouth, Massachusetts, December 22, 1802.

Happy Holidays

Whether your favorite December holiday is Christmas, Hanukkah, or the Winter Solstice, you probably give a lot of gifts. Instead of giving your cousin another tie, how about giving him something he'll enjoy all year, like an NRA membership? Perhaps instead of the usual $50 dollar check, you could give your niece something better—like your time— by taking her to the range with you once a month during the next year. Does Uncle Charlie really need more underwear? Or would he be pleasantly surprised to have a pro-rights book donated to the local public library in his name? (Most libraries will place an inscription on the inside front cover of the book to memorialize the name of the person being honored.)

Likewise, if your business regularly gives holiday presents, perhaps you could give pro-rights gifts this year. Instead of getting a fruit basket, your employees or customers might appreciate the company giving a $25 donation in their name to a group like the Second Amendment Foundation. So as not to impose upon your employees' or customers' own beliefs, you could offer each individual a choice: the gift could go to a pro-gun group, or to an alternate choice like the local United Way.

Weddings

If you already have all the toasters and cash you need, suggest that your friends make a donation to a pro-rights group in honor of your marriage

Wills

If you're reading this book, you've probably made the

determination that you can't always rely on the government to protect you and your family. So should you trust the government to take care of your family and allocate your property wisely when you're gone? Of course not. That's why you should write a will.

Wills are not only for the elderly or the wealthy. They're a simple precaution that everyone—especially everyone with dependent relatives—should take. If you write a will, you decide how your property will be distributed. If you don't write a will, the government decides. Likewise, only by writing a will can you choose who will be the guardian of your children, who will administer your estate, and who the beneficiaries will be. If you leave no will, the government will make all those choices for you, perhaps not making the choices you would have.

The best way to write a will is to get the assistance of a qualified attorney. If you have no dependents, and few assets, then a pre-printed or computer-generated standard will might work for you. But more likely, you can get the benefits of tax reduction and other advice from consulting an attorney you feel comfortable with.

To be an informed consumer of legal services, it's always best to do a little advance research on your own. As a starting point, you might want to read the NRA's free booklet "How to Protect Your Rights with a Will," which is available from: NRA, Director of Planning and Development, 12500 Waples Mill Road, Fairfax, Virginia, 22030. (703) 267-1000.

One of options you have with a will—once your dependents are well-provided for—is to leave funds to a charitable organization, such as a school, or a pro-rights group. A gift to a pro-rights group helps ensure that your loved ones—and the country you love—will have the rights that you have today.

In addition to donating money through a will, there are a variety of other ways to give assets to pro-rights organizations. For example, under Life Income Plans, you give an asset (e.g. shares in a mutual fund) to an organization. During your lifetime, you receive all the income from that asset (e.g. mutual fund dividends). After your death, the asset passes entirely to the pro-rights group. Among the benefits of Life Income Plans can be substantial tax savings.

Like most actions involving the transfer of a substantial asset, a Life Income Gift should be done in consultation with a qualified attorney.

Charitable gifts of any type, of course, do not have to be in your own name. After the death of a relative or good friend, many people give memorial gifts or set up a memorial funds, to perpetuate the memory of their loved one. The *American Rifleman* publishes contributions to Institute for Legislative Action in memory of particular individuals, as well as the name of the donor.

4. Spend Somebody Else's Money

"YOU NEED ONLY REFLECT THAT ONE OF THE BEST WAYS TO GET
YOURSELF A REPUTATION AS A DANGEROUS CITIZEN THESE DAYS
IS TO GO AROUND REPEATING THE VERY PHRASES WHICH OUR
FOUNDING FATHERS USED IN THEIR STRUGGLE FOR INDEPENDENCE."
                    —Charles A. Beard, American historian.

Gun amnesties

Did you know that you can save yourself some money
while helping to save the Second Amendment? Here are some
ways to put money in your pocket while putting the gun prohibitionists in their place.

First of all, there's probably a gun turn-in program coming to a city near you; turn in your guns, no questions asked, and
receive cash, or coupons for merchandise. This is a great opportunity to make some money by selling worthless guns.

Back in 1991, the *Oakland Press* (from Oakland, Michi-
gan) put up $10,000 in order to pay people $50 for each gun
surrendered. General (his name, not his rank) Laney, who is the
Executive Director of the Motor City Sportsmen's Association,
turned in eight junk guns and collected $400. He then told the
press that he was going to use the money to "further public education about the right to bear arms." Supporters of the gun re-
moval went nuts, and Laney remarked, "I made them look like
fools and then told the world about it. I haven't had this much fun
in a long time."

Sadly, gun turn-in programs often victimize people who
don't understand as much about gun values as does General Laney.
For instance, a widow may decide to get rid of her husband's old
hunting rifle (which will be tossed in a police furnace) in exchange
for a coupon for $75 of groceries. Unbeknownst to her, the gun
may be worth $800.

Here's where you can come in. On the day of the gun
turn-in, go the place where people are lining up. When you see

someone standing in line with an $800 rifle or other valuable gun, offer him or her a fair price for it, and pay cash on the spot. Everybody comes out ahead: the person selling the gun makes much more money by selling the gun to you, and you get a good gun at a bargain price.

Even the government/corporate officials running the gun turn-in come out ahead. By not buying the widow's $800 rifle, the gun grabbers have more money left with which to buy someone else's broken revolver that cost $14.95 when it was manufactured in 1961.

Of course be sure to comply with all relevant laws regarding firearms sales in your jurisdiction; your purchases will likely draw the attention of the local police.

Long Distance

Another way to save money is through the long distance programs offered by the National Rifle Association and by the Second Amendment Foundation.

Here's how the NRA program works. You call (800) 428-4NRA, and ask for the NRA Long Distance Advantage telephone network to become your long distance telephone carrier. Long Distance Advantage then becomes the company which transmits your long distance calls, taking the place of your present long distance carrier (such as AT&T or MCI). There is no need for any re-wiring in your home.

The long distance rates you pay are generally cheaper than the rates from the major carriers. As might be expected, discounts are best on nights and weekends.

Under the NRA basic plan, the first 60 minutes of calls you make to out-of-state numbers each week are billed at a rate of 13.9 cents per minute (for calls made nights and weekends). After the first hour of calls, the rate drops to 9.9 cents per minute.

If you typically make more than $15 or $20 of long-distance calls a month, then you can save more money by signing up for the Advantage Plus program, which costs $2.95 per month. Under the Advantage Plus system, your night and weekend out-of-state calls are billed at a straight rate of 9.9 cents per minute.

Like other long distance companies, NRA Long Distance Advantage provides you with free calling cards.

Of every dollar you spend, the National Rifle Association receives between 2% and 5%. So you spend less on long distance, and you get to steer some money to the NRA.

The program for the Second Amendment Foundation works exactly the same way. In fact, the service is (as with the NRA program), provided by the Long Distance Advantage network. The only difference between the NRA and the SAF programs is which group gets the 2% to 5% of the revenues. To sign up for the SAF program, call (800) 435-6832.

Affinity Cards

Another painless way to help the gun rights groups is to use one of their credit cards. The gun groups have agreements with the credit card issuers for the issuers to pay part of the issuer's revenues to the gun rights groups. (Credit card issuers, such as banks, make money from 1. charging fees to merchants that accept the credit cards; 2. interest on unpaid balances; 3. annual fees to card-holders).

The Visa card for NRA members has no annual fee. (Most credit cards impose an annual fee after the first year.)

The NRA Visa card is issued by a company called Credit Card Plan. You can receive an application for the card by calling (800) 786-4672. You need to be an NRA member to receive the card, and you can call the same number to join the NRA. Of course normal credit application procedures apply for the NRA Visa card, as with any other credit card.

An additional advantage of using the NRA Visa card is that you provide free advertising for the gun rights movement every time you use the card. Waiters, gas station attendants, store clerks, and everybody else who processes your card will see someone who is proud of belonging to the largest civil rights organization in the United States.

The Second Amendment Foundation has its own credit

card program, with a card that is more expensive than the NRA Visa card, but might suit your needs better. The SAF Mastercard is issued by the MBNA company, which can be contacted at (800) 847-7378.

MBNA cards typically have a large number of bonus features not offered by competing credit cards. For example the basic SAF Mastercard includes $300,000 of travel insurance when you buy airplane tickets with the card, and also includes Collision Damage Waiver insurance for automobile rentals.

You can also get a Gold SAF Mastercard, which includes more features, the best of which is a warranty extension for products you buy with the card.

The interest rate on the SAF cards are variable, and are currently 15.9%. If you transfer a balance from another credit card over to the SAF card, you pay only 9.9% on the transfer balance. (Rates fluctuate constantly, so check the latest rates when if you decide to apply.)

The cards have no annual fee for the first year. Thereafter, the basic card costs $20 a year, and the annual card costs $40 a year. (The NRA Visa card has no annual fee, but an 18% interest rate, with a balance-transfer rate of 11.5%).

Of course you do not need to belong to the Second Amendment Foundation to apply for these cards.

More NRA Discounts

National Car Rental offers reduced rates to NRA members. Call 800-CAR-RENT, and give them "NRA Service no. 5130054."

North American Van Lines gives NRA members a 40% discount on interstate moves, plus $50,000 of free moving insurance. Call (800) 245-6895 ext. 29.

5. Tax Deductions

"HE HAS ERECTED A MULTITUDE OF NEW OFFICES AND SENT HITHER SWARMS OF OFFICERS TO HARASS OUR PEOPLE, AND EAT OUT THEIR SUBSTANCE."
—Thomas Jefferson, *The Declaration of Independence*, listing the abuses of King George III

What's your favorite thing about paying taxes? Some folks like the handy payroll deduction system, whereby Uncle Sam helps himself to your money every time you get paid. Payroll deduction was instituted during World War II, supposedly as a "temporary" measure. Payroll deduction has stayed permanent, however, since the federal government prefers to take your money in little bits; the feds know that trying to collect today's high taxes in one lump sum on April 15 would cause a massive tax revolt.

My favorite part of the tax system, however, is how efficiently the federal government uses our tax dollars. For instance, in Paris in January 1993, the United States government signed the Chemical Weapons Convention treaty, which outlawed the use of certain chemical warfare agents in international warfare. Although the treaty was probably a good idea, the federal government was left with a problem: the government already had a plentiful supply of CS chemical warfare agent, which was now illegal to use against hostile armies.

Did the federal government waste your taxes dollars by throwing away the now-illegal chemical warfare agent? Of course not. The government found an alternative use.

Rather than let the internationally-banned CS chemical warfare agent go to waste, our federal government used the agent against American children, who (unlike foreign soldiers) were not protected by the Chemical Weapons Convention.

As you may recall, on February 28, 1993, the Bureau of Alcohol, Tobacco and Firearms had served a search warrant by breaking into and shooting at a religious community in Waco,

Texas. The BATF had explained that service of the search warrant with an armed assault was necessary because the children in the compound were in danger, because some of the adults in the compound had allegedly built machine guns without getting prior permission from the federal government.

The initial attempt to protect the children was not successful, and a siege ensued. During the siege, the federal government cut off electricity, fired "flash-bang" devices at persons who attempted to leave the building, shined klieg lights on the building all night to prevent anyone in the building from sleeping, and blasted ear-splitting tape recordings of rabbits being slaughtered and other pleasant noises. Telephone lines were cut, and people in the compound were prevented from talking with anyone except government agents; in particular, family members were not allowed to talk with persons inside the compound.

After several weeks of government-enforced isolation, psychological warfare, and no electricity, the federal agents (all paid with your tax dollars), determined that "the children were living in a deteriorating environment."

The federal government then devised plan to rescue the children from the "deteriorating environment." The plan consisted of sending tanks to destroy the children's home, and pumping it full of the CS chemical warfare agent. Although the CS agent could not legally have been used against invading Cuban paratroopers, it was used legally against the children (since they weren't foreign soldiers); and thus the government prevented the waste of chemical warfare supplies bought at taxpayer expense.

A few hours later, all of the children were burned to death by a massive fire as they huddled with their mothers in a concrete room in the center of the house. The tanks (your tax dollars at work) had so thoroughly destroyed the house that all the exits the children and their mothers might have used were blocked.

The Bureau of Alcohol, Tobacco and Firearms then hoisted a white and blue "ATF" flag over the smoldering remains of the compound. The bodies of the children, whom the federal government had so earnestly tried to protect from child abuse, lay dead.

There are better things to do than turn over your hard-earned income to the federal government to finance such child abuse programs. For instance, you can give some of your money to groups that support the right to keep and bear arms. By giving money to a tax-exempt, pro-rights foundation, you reduce your taxes, and ensure that your money is used for a better purpose than chemical warfare attacks on toddlers.

One good, tax-exempt group is the Firearms Civil Rights Legal Defense Fund, located at 12500 Waples Mill Road, Fairfax, Virginia 22030. The FCRLDF supports litigation and research on behalf of the right to keep and bear arms and the right to self defense.

A typical FCRLDF case was that of Louis Gatti. When Gatti used a handgun to capture an escaped mental patient and two other criminals who had broken into his family's Washington, D.C. property, he should have been given a medal. Instead, he was prosecuted for possessing a pistol without a license. A Virginia resident temporarily in Washington, Gatti had not realized that his handgun (which he legally owned under Virginia law), was illegal in Washington.

The charge for possessing an unlicensed handgun was particularly outrageous since Washington bureaucrats never give handgun licenses to ordinary citizens.

Happily, Gatti was acquitted, thanks to legal assistance provided by the Firearms Civil Rights Legal Defense Fund. The fund supports scores of cases throughout the United States which help individual citizens and create important legal precedents protecting gun owners.

Notably, federal employees may make automatic payroll donations to the FCRLDF through the Combined Federal Campaign. Anyone else who participates in the United Way Combined Campaign at work can designate the Firearms Civil Rights Legal Defense Fund for their donation. Even if the donation form does not specifically list the FCRLDF as a recipient group, you can write in the group's name and address, and the money will go to it. If you have any questions about designating a United Way contribution to the FCRLDF, call FCRLDF Secretary Robert Dowlut at 703-267-1254. You can also make credit card donations by calling 703-267-1068.

Although the FCRLDF is a separate entity from the National Rifle Association, the FCRLDF works closely with the NRA in implementing effective litigation strategies.

Another place to give money is the NRA Foundation. The NRA Foundation funds the Eddie Eagle Gun Safety program (which has taught basic gun safety to over four million children); hunter safety education; Partners in Shooting (to help disabled people participate in the shooting sports); as well as other programs involving youth and adult marksmanship training and range development. You can earmark donations for a specific NRA Foundation program if you wish.

The NRA also has a National Firearms Museum Fund (to support the National Firearms Museum, now located in Fairfax, Virginia); and the NRA Special Contribution Fund (supporting the NRA shooting center in Whittington, New Mexico).

You can give to any of the NRA funds by sending a check made out to the particular fund to: NRA, Office of the Treasurer, 11250 Waples Mill Road, Fairfax, Virginia, 22030. Or you can make a credit card donation by calling 703-267-1133. If you participate in a United Way Campaign, you can designate the NRA Foundation for your donations; if you need help filling out the designation form, call the NRA Foundation at 703-267-1133.

(Note: federal employees participating in the Combined Federal Campaign are currently allowed to donate to the Firearms Civil Rights Legal Defense Fund, but not to the NRA Foundation, which is too new to qualify for the Combined Federal Campaign. But again, if you participate in a regular United Way campaign, you can donate to the NRA Foundation).

Besides the Foundations affiliated with the National Rifle Association, there are two other national foundations worth noting.

The Second Amendment Foundation supports education and legal projects related to the right to keep and bear arms. Lawsuits brought by SAF have thrown out handgun bans in San Francisco and New Haven, and have forced the Los Angeles Police

Department to begin issuing handgun carry permits to people who have been threatened.

A couple years ago, SAF attorneys successfully argued a case before the Washington State Supreme Court that overturned a law that revoked firearms rights from individuals who had been evaluated by mental health officials—even if the individuals were found not to be mentally ill.

The Second Amendment Foundation is located at 12500 N.E. Tenth Place, Bellevue, Wash. 98005. (206) 454-7012. You can join SAF for $15 a year, or become a life member for $100. Again, all contributions are tax deductible.

Finally, there's the Gun Owners Foundation. This Foundation, related to Gun Owners of America, also participates in the Combined Federal Campaign. The Foundation has helped many gun dealers and other citizens defend themselves against unfair Bureau of Alcohol, Tobacco and Firearms prosecutions. Gun Owners Foundation also publishes educational material, including books and videotapes. 8001 Forbes Place, Suite 102, Springfield, VA 22151. (703) 321-8585.

The Gun Owners Foundation participates in the Combined Federal Campaign. Both the Second Amendment Foundation and the Gun Owners Foundation can be designated as your recipient when you participate in a United Way campaign.

Many companies have matching gift programs. If your employer does, ask if it will match a gift to any of these organizations, all of which have been IRS approved as tax-exempt charitable organizations.

Lastly, many folks who make a special donation to a charitable group make the donation in memory of someone special who has passed away, such as an uncle who taught them how to shoot, a buddy who served in combat with them, or a favorite teacher. Perhaps you could make your next donation to a pro-rights foundation in memory of the children at Waco who were killed by the federal government. The more resources you shift from the federal ledger to the pro-rights ledger, the better our chances to prevent the tax-sponsored murder of little boys and girls.

6. Investments

"BOTH OLIGARCH AND TYRANT MISTRUST THE PEOPLE, AND
THEREFORE DEPRIVE THEM OF ARMS." —Aristotle

One way to invest your money with a pro-rights group is to put it in the NRA's Reserve Fund U.S. Government Portfolio. The portfolio consists entirely of short-term U.S. Government obligations. There is a $1,000 minimum initial investment. You can make withdrawals ($500 minimum) by check or by telephone. The fund has over three billion dollars in assets. The number to call to receive a prospectus is (800) 223-5547.

Of course some folks, quite understandably, don't like lending money to a government run by Bill Clinton and similar "friends" of the Constitution. A good alternative investment for such folks is the Bank of Boulder.

This Bank has a special Certificate of Deposit program. When you buy a CD, you get an NRA membership. If you're already a member, you can give the membership to a family member or a friend.

Normally, a Certificate of Deposit pays interest in dribs and drabs over the life of the CD. The Bank of Boulder CD, however, gives you all your interest up front. And you get the interest not in the form of cash, but instead as a new Browning or Weatherby rifle or shotgun, or fishing equipment.

Making the deal even better, your taxable liability for the interest does not come due all at once when you receive the rifle or shotgun. The tax liability is spread over the full term of the CD. Every year, the Bank will send you a 1099 INT form detailing your imputed interest for that year.

The Bank of Boulder has signed up many thousands of new NRA members, and given away over 10,000 rifles and shotguns through this program. The Bank is located at 3033 Iris Ave., Boulder, CO 80301. Even if you live outside of Colorado, you can still buy a CD from the Bank; the gun will be shipped to a licensed firearms dealer in your home state, so that you can take possession of the gun.

The Bank's excellent CD program aggravates the anti-gun lobby to no end, which is another reason to support this excellent, pro-gun bank.

7. Friends of NRA

"POWER, WHETHER VESTED IN THE MANY OR A FEW, IS EVER
GRASPING, AND, LIKE THE GRAVE, CRIES, "GIVE, GIVE!"
—Abigail Adams, Revolutionary War patriot, and wife of John
Adams

Finally (since this is the last part of the "financial" section), if you're really committed to helping to steer money towards the cause of freedom, one great thing you can do is help arrange a Friends of NRA program.

Friends of NRA events, usually held in the evening, draw crowds of 200 to 800 Americans who want to participate in a pro-gun event. The evening's events can include a banquet, an auction of collector's item firearms, and speeches by national NRA leaders. The events are also a great opportunity for an area's pro-gun activists to get together—and to help get other gun owners in the area a little more active.

The money from the event goes to the tax-deductible NRA Foundation. Half the money stays in your home state for programs such as range development and firearms safety education; the other half goes towards national programs.

Putting on a Friends of NRA event is too much work for a single person, but with a group of committed volunteers, it can be a lot of fun. Happily, since the Friends program has been running for a while now, the NRA can supply you with detailed directions and plenty of assistance for a smooth event, from planning, to publicity, to the day itself.

If you're interested in helping with a Friends of NRA event, talk to your NRA Field Representative. If you don't know who your field rep is, call the Field Services Division at NRA headquarters (703-267-1354).

Part II

Communications and Education

In our last book, we gave lots of advice about how to educate yourself on the gun issue, and how to pass that education on to the public. Here are some more tips about how to spread accurate information regarding our right to keep and bear arms.

The reason that we come back to the education issue in this book is because it's so important. In the long run, helping the public learn the truth about firearms and the Second Amendment is the most important thing you can do to defend our rights. The lobbying of the anti-gun organizations can only succeed if legislators and the public have first been softened up by anti-gun propaganda. In the long run, the preservation of the Second Amendment will depend much less on the abilities of Washington lobbyists than on how hard and how effectively pro-rights activists work at winning the hearts and minds of the American people.

8. *Fight Back Against Media Bias*

"THEY TELL US WE ARE WEAK—UNABLE TO COPE WITH SO FOR-MIDABLE AN ADVERSARY. BUT WHEN SHALL BE WE STRONGER? WILL IT BE NEXT WEEK, OR THE NEXT YEAR? WILL IT BE WHEN WE ARE TOTALLY DISARMED? SHALL WE ACQUIRE THE MEANS OF EFFECTUAL RESISTANCE BY LYING SUPINELY ON OUR BACKS AND HUGGING THE DELUSIVE PHANTOM OF HOPE, UNTIL OUR ENEMIES HAVE BOUND US HAND AND FOOT?

WE ARE NOT WEAK IF WE MAKE A PROPER USE OF THE MEANS WHICH THE GOD OF NATURE HAS PLACED IN OUR POWER. MILLIONS OF PEOPLE ARMED IN THE HOLY CAUSE OF LIBERTY, AND IN SUCH A COUNTRY AS THAT WHICH WE POSSESS, ARE IN-VINCIBLE. BESIDES, WE SHALL NOT FIGHT OUR BATTLES ALONE. THERE IS A JUST GOD WHO PRESIDES OVER THE DESTINIES OF NATIONS, WHO WILL RAISE UP FRIENDS TO FIGHT OUR BATTLES FOR US. THE BATTLE IS NOT TO THE STRONG ALONE; IT IS TO THE VIGILANT, THE ACTIVE, THE BRAVE.

MANY CRY 'PEACE, PEACE'—BUT THERE IS NO PEACE. THE WAR IS ACTUALLY BEGUN! WHY STAND WE HERE IDLE? IS LIFE SO DEAR, OR PEACE SO SWEET, AS TO BE PURCHASED AT THE PRICE OF CHAINS AND SLAVERY. FORBID IT ALMIGHTY GOD! I KNOW NOT WHAT COURSE OTHERS MAY TAKE; BUT AS FOR ME, GIVE ME LIBERTY OR GIVE ME DEATH!"

—Patrick Henry.

Media bias against gun owners keeps getting worse. Net-work entertainment, while glorifying violence, condemns lawful gun ownership. Network infotainment (the descendent of old-fash-ioned "news") relies on anti-gun talking heads such as Connie Chung and Tom Brokaw who present as "news" based on the latest press releases from the gun prohibition lobby.

Media executives are getting increasingly sophisticated about slipping Sarah Brady's party line everywhere. For example, in a February 1994 segment of NYPD Blue (a supposedly realis-tic police drama), the police interrogating some teenagers with illegal guns slipped in several lines about how the kids had gone down to West Virginia to buy the guns. Of course the Gun Control Act of 1968 makes it illegal in West Virginia, just like everywhere else in the United States, for a gun store to sell a handgun to a person under 21. That little fact, of course, never made it into the "realistic" program.

Does all this make you feel helpless, like you might as well just give up, bury a couple guns, and hand the rest over to the government? Well, don't fold so easily.

Remember that the core of the gun prohibition lobbies' strength has always been from the media. As a genuine citizen movement, the gun prohibition lobbies are insignificant, having few donors, and even fewer volunteers. But the gun prohibitionists know how to leverage their influence; through adroit placement of stories in sympathetic media, the prohibitionists create the false impression that there is a great national outcry for repressive gun laws.

Moreover, the giant media outlets—and their sponsors—are susceptible to citizen influence. The television industry hates gun-owners, because such hatred is part of the commonly-accepted bigotry of the industry's social milieu. But concern about the gun issue (or any other issue), is dwarfed by an obsession with profits. The entertainment and infotainment divisions of CBS television may have little regard for truth, but they have a tremendous regard for the bottom line.

When the networks receive a heavy volume of letters complaining about bias on a television program, the networks will sometimes back off. If you have an opinion about a particular program or series, here's where to write or call:

NBC Television
30 Rockefeller Plaza
New York, NY 10122
(212) 664-4444

CBS Television
51 W. 52d St.
New York, NY 10019
(212) 975-3247

ABC Television
1330 Avenue of the Americas
New York, NY 10019
(212) 887-7777

Home Box Office (HBO)
Consumer Affairs
1100 Avenue of the Americas
New York, NY 10036
(212) 512-1000

Cable News Network (CNN)
Box 105366
One CNN Center
Atlanta, GA 30348
(404) 827-1000

Fox
PO Box 900
Beverly Hills, CA 90213

National Public Radio
2025 M St. NW
Washington, DC 20036
(800) 235-1212

(We know, NPR is radio rather than TV, but their coverage of the gun issue is even more dishonest than the coverage from network television.)

Notice anything interesting about the addresses for these folks? NBC, ABC, CBS, and HBO are within a few blocks of each other on the West Side of New York City. What's it like over there? Well, leftist feminist Betty Friedan (who lives on the West Side), once exclaimed that she couldn't understand how Reagan had won the 1984 election, since she didn't know anybody who had voted for him.

Although the television producers fancy themselves to be very worldly and sophisticated, they often reflect the shallow elitist attitudes of their West Side social set. Since they don't know anyone who owns a semi-automatic, or enjoys target shooting with a revolver, they figure that anyone who does must be some kind of paranoid nut.

NRA Media Monitor

There are two other important groups who need to receive your complaints about media bias.

All local broadcast stations must have their licenses renewed every few years by the Federal Communications Commission. At license renewal time, a documented record of bias hurts the station. Even if it doesn't result in the license being canceled (cancellations are very rare), the more that media executives have to squirm during the renewal process, the more careful they will be in the next few years.

So when you see bias on local television programming, send a letter to the Federal Communications Commission, Mass Media Bureau, 1919 M St. NW, Washington, DC 20036. Explain in the letter the date and time of the biased or dishonest broadcast, the station's call letters, the program name and format, and who told the lie or made the biased comment. Let the FCC know that you think the coverage was unfair, and that you respectfully request your letter be placed in the station's file.

Send a copy of your letter to Media Monitor, NRA General Counsel, 11250 Waples Mill Road, Fairfax VA 22030. When license renewal time comes, the NRA will be able to use all the letters compiled from people like you to document a station's repeated policy of bias and distortion.

Sponsors

Letters to a show's sponsors are often more effective than a letter to the network itself. Sponsors are, after all, interested in selling their product, not getting potential customers mad at them. For information on contacting corporations which have sponsored anti-gun programs, see chapter 2.

Media Bias Guide

Lastly, if you really want to educate yourself about tackling media bias, get a copy of *How to Identify, Expose, & Correct Liberal Media Bias*, by Brent H. Baker. This 300 page book is published by the Media Research Center, Publications Dept., 113 South West St., Alexandria, VA 22312. (703) 683-9733.

This book teaches you how to analyze news stories, and how to conduct research testing for the existence of bias. Baker identifies eight categories of bias: by commission, by omission, by placement, by story selection, by selection of sources, by spin, by labeling, and by policy recommendation. Although the book's slant is anti-liberal, the lessons you learn here will also help you identify conservative bias.

The book includes an appendix that lists newspaper and television addresses, and also various conservative publications and organizations.

9. Citizen Replies to Television Editorials

"GOOD INTENTIONS WILL ALWAYS BE PLEADED FOR EVERY AS-
SUMPTION FOR AUTHORITY. IT IS HARDLY TOO STRONG TO SAY
THAT THE CONSTITUTION WAS MADE TO GUARD THE PEOPLE
AGAINST THE DANGERS OF GOOD INTENTIONS. THERE ARE MEN
IN ALL AGES WHO MEAN TO GOVERN WELL, BUT THEY MEAN TO
GOVERN. THEY PROMISE TO BE GOOD MASTERS, BUT THEY MEAN
TO BE MASTERS."
—Senator Daniel Webster of New Hampshire.

Although no longer required by law, some television stations still allow citizens to present on-the-air replies to television
editorials. Be prepared to be persistent and polite in calling back
and asking the station for a decision. And remember, any opportunity you are offered is strictly a gift from the station, not a legal
obligation.

If the station does let you on the air, here's how to pro-
ceed:

· Keep your statement to a length of 60 seconds or less.
· Practice over and over till you're very comfortable with it.
· Wear a business suit.
· Get a nice haircut, and be trim and tidy. (This is show busi-
ness, and how you look affects people's willingness to listen
to what you have to say.)
· Smile and be friendly.
· Mention only enough about the station's editorial so that view-
ers can remember what you're talking about.
· Focus less on rebutting the station's editorial than on present-
ing our own positive case.
· Write a memorable closing line that summarizes your posi-
tion.

The same tips that apply to letters to the editor, op-ed pieces,
letters to elected officials, and talk radio (all discussed in our first

book) apply here too: don't engage in personal accusations; don't present conspiracy theories; and always show by your good behavior how responsible gun owners really are.

10. More Media Tips

"WHOEVER USES FORCE WITHOUT RIGHT...PUTS HIMSELF INTO A STATE OF WAR WITH THOSE, AGAINST WHOM HE USES IT, AND IN THAT STATE ALL FORMER TIES ARE CANCELED, ALL OTHER RIGHTS CEASE, AND EVERY ONE HAS A RIGHT TO DEFEND HIMSELF, AND TO RESIST THE AGGRESSOR."

—John Locke

Publicity

In our previous book (*Things You Can Do to Defend Your Gun Rights*), we talked about how to write a press release, conduct a press conference, and generate favorable pro-rights media attention. If you're interested in learning more about these topics, there are two books we recommend.

First is *Publicity for Volunteers: A Handbook*, by Virginia Boron (New York: Walker, 1981). The book is written especially for folks who run community organizations and who have no prior experience with media. The book takes you through press releases, public service announcements, newsletters, event planning, and much more. If you are doing public relations for a local pro-rights group, every minute you spend reading this book will save you hours of time by making your efforts more efficient.

The other book is *Prime Time Activism: Media Strategies for Grassroots Organizing*, by Charlotte Ryan (Boston: South End Press, 1991). This book moves beyond the nuts-and-bolts approach of *Publicity for Volunteers* to focus on the special problem of groups which represent a viewpoint outside the mainstream media propaganda machine. The book details how the media "frame" reality in order to exclude viewpoints they dislike. The book then explains how "challengers" can work with the media to help the media frame the story more accurately.

The "frame" of the book's author is a leftist one; to illustrate her point, she uses stories such as a hotel workers' strike in Boston and U.S. intervention in Nicaragua. But her points about how "challengers" need to cast their stories to get the mainstream media to pay attention are valid for persons of all ideological viewpoints.

Adopt a Reporter

Personal experience aside, reporters are people, too. They respond to others. The Citizens Committee for the Right to Keep and Bear Arms has a simple program to "Adopt A Reporter" who covers gun issues and get to know him or her—while letting the reporter get to know you, too. It won't change the reporter's approach to reporting—they like to think they are always professional and objective even when they're spouting the most biased opinion, but that's just human nature. "Adopting" a reporter means keeping track of the reporter's coverage: reading the newspaper or magazine regularly, looking for stories by your "adopted" reporter, reading them carefully, and responding to each one. The idea is to promote familiarity with the issue. When an "adopted" reporter does a good or bad job, let them know. A telephone call, letter, fax or e-mail message is all it takes. And at some point, you might even arrange a personal meeting. Put a human face on your issue—yours.

Publish a Newspaper

With the help of Gun Owners of America, you can put out a four-page gun rights newsletter exposing the voting record of an anti-gun legislator who claims to be pro-gun. Such a newspaper can be quite cheap to print—as little as three cents per copy.

These newspapers are a great way to put the heat on the elected who have broken their promise to oppose restrictions on the Second Amendment. You can hand out the newspaper at gun shows and gun stores, and mail it to local groups of gun owners. To find out more about how to print such a newspaper (and get plenty of help in doing so), contact Erich Pratt at Gun Owners of America, 8001 Forbes Place, Suite 102, Springfield, VA 22151. (703) 321-8585.

NRA Guide

The NRA has published a short "Guide to Media Interviews" which provides excellent tips in handling various types of questions. Call the NRA Institute at Office at (703) 267-1190 for a copy.

11. CD-Roms

"HERE I AM; SEND ME."

—Isaiah 6:8

An excellent CD-ROM is *The Gun Rights Compendium: Ammunition for the Gun Rights Activist.* Created by Leroy Pyle, founder of the Paul Revere Network (discussed in the next chapter), the CD contains over 1,500 files of important Second Amendment information. It also includes the full text of J. Neil Schulman's excellent book *Stopping Power* (described in chapter 13). You'll find sample letters for activists, gun software, statistics, legislation relating to guns, the full text of Supreme Court decisions related to the Second Amendment, short and long articles by numerous authors (including a good number from Dave), and much more.

If all this sounds like the full information bank from a highly-quality pro-gun computer bulletin board, that's exactly what it is. As a CD, *The Gun Rights Compendium* does not contain new material after the CD's July 1994 release, but it is still incredibly valuable.

There is, however, a caveat. *The Gun Rights Compendium* does not include its own graphical interface. The CD is essentially a huge collection of files, organized in a directory tree. To search and read the files, you'll need your own word processing program (which as a computer owner, you almost certainly have).

Without a graphical interface, the way you look for files is by browsing through the directory tree. The filenames, like all DOS filenames, are no more than 11 characters long, which can make some titles awfully obscure. Still, the extra effort necessary for working your way through this incredible database is well worth it. $54.95, plus $5.00 shipping and handling. The Paul Revere Network, 666 N. Second St., San Jose, CA 95112. (408) 292-2790.

12. Computer Bulletin Boards and other Electronic Communication

> "AND THE RIFLE? WON'T GO OUT NAKED OF A RIFLE. WHEN
> SHOES AND CLOTHES AND FOOD, WHEN EVEN HOPE IS GONE,
> WE'LL HAVE THE RIFLE."
> —John Steinbeck, *The Grapes of Wrath*

Gun Rights Computer Bulletin Boards

Our last book sang the praises of computer bulletin boards, and everything we said then is true today, only double. Tanya Metaksa is not exaggerating too greatly when she says you can't be an activist unless you have a computer, and if you don't have a modem, you don't have a computer.

The change that computer communications are effecting on the gun control debate is tremendously significant. As long as the Rathers and Brokaws of the world turn HCI press releases into "news" stories, the impression exists that (a.) informed opinion and (b.) the public in general is in agreement with the HCI general agenda. But in the long run, electronic communications have begun to revolutionize politics. The massive increase in electronic communications (the NRA board, the more than 150 Paul Revere echo boards, Internet, the gun stuff on almost every major commercial service) is already playing a major role in empowering gun rights supporters by (1.) making them realize that there are plenty of other people who think the way they do, and (2.) exposing them to additional information (pro and con) which (a.) ultimately confirms the pro-rights position, and (b.) makes them more articulate.

The number of people who discuss public policy on BBSs is pretty small, compared to the general population. But the number of *New Republic* readers compared to the general population is small too. BBS folks are opinion leaders.

The anti-gun movement only exists as a substantial political force now because of its adept leveraging of the opinion/information elite's general prejudice about guns. Under current conditions, if you control the dominant organs of public opinion (the northeastern seaboard media), then you control a lot of what people think. BBSs are part of a revolution that is changing all that. When people can download a copy of the federal health care bill, then what NBC News chooses to tell people about health care becomes less important.

If the Stockton shootings happened today, the political impact would have been much different. Now there is a network of hundreds of thousands of pro-rights BBS users who, within 48 hours, would know more about the actual facts than the editors of most newspapers. Whatever play the story got in the media (including the false claims that the gun used was a machine gun, and that machine guns can be bought over the counter), plenty of folks who were talking about the story would have a much better chance (compared to that in 1989) of conversing with someone who, thanks to electronic communications systems like BBS, had a vastly different and more accurate understanding of the event than the person reliant on the dominant media.

The fact that the pro-rights side is doing so well on the BBSs is indicative of a major power shift away from the gun prohibition movement. There are plenty of other things that may help the antis prosper in coming decades, but electronic communications is destined to become a tremendous barrier to the antis' political success.

Internet

If you use the Internet, you know the wealth of information at your fingertips. It's the information bullseye for gun rights advocates. In fact, you can read the first volume of *Things You Can Do to Defend Your Gun Rights* by simply dialing and signing on. You can also access Supreme Court decisions since 1970, law review journals, back issues of the Gottlieb-Tartaro Report and other timely materials with the click of a button.

You can get aboard via World Wide Web, File Transefer Protocol (FTP) or Gopher. These interfaces are available from local providers, as well as the big boys: Compuserve, America Online, Prodigy, etc.

Second Amendment Foundation can be reached at ftp.saf.org or www.saf.org or via gopher.

National Rifle Association can be reached at ftp.nra.org or www.nra.org or via gopher.

You can get electronically delivered copies of press releases and action alerts by simply sending email messages to Second Amendment Foundation and National Rifle Association. The message for alerts should read SUBSCRIBE RKBA-ALERT *YOUR FULL NAME* and sent to LISTPROC@SAF.ORG for SAF and LISTPROC@NRA.ORG for the NRA. You can receive press release by sending a message SUBSCRIBE PRESS RELEASE *YOUR FULL NAME* to the same places. If you get stuck just type in help! and send it to LISTSERV@SAF.ORG or LISTSERV@NRA.ORG.

You can also locate the latest versions of federal legislation by connecting to THOMAS@LOC.GOV, the Library of Congress' congressional information.

The best thing of all is that there is no charge for the information, just your regular phone costs—usually local lines only.

Gun Talk

If all the Internet stuff is Greek to you, don't worry. You can get everything in NRA.ORG, and much, much more, by connecting to the NRA's "Gun Talk" computer bulletin board. Just have your modem dial (703) 934-2121. (Settings are the usual N-8-1.) Have your NRA membership number handy, and you'll be on your way to an incredible treasure of gun news reports (updated several times a day), research files, reloading programs, and lots more. If you can afford the long-distance phone charges, Gun Talk is definitely the premier source for electronic information.

E-Mail

Many congressional offices now have access to electronic mail systems such as the Internet. This means that you can send a message to Congress that will arrive much faster than postal mail. This immediate access can be especially crucial when legislation is moving fast, and there may not be time for a regular letter to get to Washington. (In such emergencies, folks without a modem can just give the legislator a phone call.)

To get an Internet connection to Congress, send a message to the Congressional host administrator, Doreen Albiston. Her address is dalbisto@HR.HOUSE.GOV. If you're having trouble communicating, you can also send in a request to House Information Systems, H2-627 Ford House Office Building, Washington, DC 20515, or call (202) 226-6176. Whatever format you decide to communicate in, include your e-mail mailing address, your postal (geographic) address, and also you state and zip code; this will ensure that your messages will be sent to your own representative.

The White House is also open for electronic mail. The addresses are: PRESIDENT@WHITEHOUSE.GOV, and VICE.PRESIDENT@WHITEHOUSE.GOV.

NRA Fax Alert

If you have a fax machine, you can receive updates on national, state, and local legislation. Timely faxes let you know exactly who to call or contact as legislation proceeds. To get on the NRA fax list, call NRA Grassroots at (800) 392-8683.

Telephone Hotlines

In the previous book, we published a list of telephone hotlines for staying up-to-date on national and local gun issues. One new number is:

Western Missouri Shooters' Alliance: (816) 229-7350.

13. More Good Reading

"WITHOUT LOVE IN YOUR DREAM IT'LL NEVER COME TRUE."

—Robert Hunter

Our first book listed many excellent books about the gun control debate. The more you read, the better you will be able to help you friends and neighbors think clearly about the gun issue. Here are some fine new books published in the last couple years.

One of the most positive developments for the long-term future of the Second Amendment has been the proliferation of books and scholarly articles which take the pro-rights side. Any of these books will be worthwhile reading, depending on your particular interests. Every one of these books should be purchased and donated to a local public library or school library. As a library book, these volumes can enlighten dozens of people, especially students, about the right to arms. For the long-run preservation of our Constitutional rights, donating pro-rights books to libraries is one of the most effective things you can do.

Assuming that your local library is a tax-exempt organization (and virtually all public libraries and school libraries are), your donation of the book is tax-deductible, based on the value of the book.

Stopping Power

The first recommended book is J. Neil Schulman's *Stopping Power*. An award-winning science fiction writer, Schulman has penned a well-written, forcefully argued explanation of why gun ownership by good people enhances public safety.

The book is a collection of essays that Schulman has written over the last several years. Some of the essays were first printed in the *Los Angeles Times*, while others have shown up on computer bulletin boards and similar places. Many of the essays deal with the meaning of the Second Amendment, and why ordinary folks should be allowed to carry a gun for protection.

The carry issue is of particular importance in the nation-wide gun debate these days. Following the lead of 22 other states, many states are debating whether to enact laws that allow licensed, trained citizens who pass a background check to obtain a permit to carry a handgun. Schulman persuasively shows that such laws—rather than turning a state into "the wild west"—actually enhance the safety of everyone—including people who don't choose to carry a gun.

Schulman's writing style is clear, and fun to read. The straight-forward writing and the short chapters make *Stopping Power* is a good first book for people who want to learn more about the gun issue. *Stopping Power* is also an excellent choice for your friends who are anti-gun, but who have enough intellectual curiosity to want to check out the argument in favor of gun ownership. By the time they're finished with *Stopping Power*, they may well have decided to switch sides.

Stopping Power can be obtained by going to your local bookstore. Since the store probably won't have a copy in stock, you can ask the store to do a "special order." (There is almost never any surcharge for this.) The store will call a book wholesaler, who will ship *Stopping Power* to the store, and you can have your copy in a few days or a few weeks. (Same procedure applies for ordering the other books discussed here.) In addition, you can phone-order a copy of *Stopping Power* directly from the publisher (310-829-2752; Visa, MC, Discover, and American Express all accepted), or from the Second Amendment Foundation (206-454-7012).

Schulman's book, by the way, reflects another trend which bodes quite well for the future of the Second Amendment: the rise of desktop publishing. Schulman produced the master pages for the book on his home computer. The book is beautifully laid out, with a very clean and inviting presentation. As personal computers demonopolize the establishment media's ability to control the distribution of information, more and more people will learn the truth about guns, as opposed to the agitprop from the establishment media.

Moreover, computers are empowering. People who know that they are competent to handle complex tools like computers are less likely to swallow the gun prohibition lobbies' claim that Americans are too stupid and unskilled to be able to handle simple (but dangerous) tools like guns.

Legal History

For the last decade, readers in search of a legal history of the Second Amendment have often turned to Stephen Halbrook's *That Every Man Be Armed.* This book, which has been reprinted by the Liberty Tree Network (800-927-873) sells for $16.95 in paperback. There is also a nine-volume cassette tape series based on the book ($49.95, from Liberty Tree Network.)

As Halbrook would be the first to admit, however, there has been a great deal of new research about the Second Amendment in the last decade. While *That Every Man Be Armed* is a fine starting point for Second Amendment legal history, the most thorough book-size analysis of the legal history of the right to arms in America is a new book by Clayton Cramer, *For the Defense of Themselves and the State: The Original Intent Judicial Interpretation of the Right to Keep and Bear Arms.* Selling for $49.95, *For the Defense of Themselves and the State* is produced by the respected academic publishing house Praeger, from Westport, Connecticut. You can special order a copy from your local bookstore, or you can call the publisher directly, at 800-225-5800.

After a short chapter on the European origins of the right to keep and bear arms, Cramer plunges into a detailed analysis of the legal history of the Second Amendment, and of the treatment of the right to bear arms in state and federal courts over the following 200 years.

One particularly important contribution made by Cramer is his detailed analysis of gun control cases in the state courts in the 19th century. Judicial hostility to the right to bear arms, Cramer shows us, is nothing new. Intellectual dishonesty, mistrust of ordinary people, and sometimes outright lying have characterized the approach of much of the judiciary to the right to bear arms since 1820s. Not all state courts have been willing to use illogical, legal "reasoning" to undermine the right to arms, but many have. As Cramer explicates, judicial contortions have been especially noticeable in slave-holding states. When legislatures have attempted to degrade (or even destroy entirely) the right to *bear* arms, too many courts have refused to intervene.

To be sure, Cramer also discusses the many state court decisions from Georgia, Washington, and elsewhere in which courts have upheld their oath to enforce the Constitution, and have struck down laws aimed at gun-owners.

But as the reader follows Cramer's narrative from the dawn of the Second Amendment up to the present, the conclusion is inevitable: relying solely on the courts to protect our gun rights is a fatal error. The problem with the courts is not that the federal and state Constitutional provisions regarding the right to keep and bear arms are ambiguous. To the contrary, courts which want to avoid enforcing Constitutional arms rights guarantees often have to perform amazing linguistic tricks. The core problem is that the judiciary is generally socially conservative, elitist, and frightened of the idea of an armed populace.

For the Defense of Themselves and the State shows clearly that if you want the Second Amendment to be protected, you're going to have to get politically involved, and do the protecting yourself. Generally speaking, the courts won't do it for you.

Too often, scholars who write about legal topics get trapped in legal arcana, and end up producing a book that can be read only by legal specialists. Cramer, to his great credit, succeeds in making legal cases comprehensible to the ordinary reader, and treating legal cases with the subtlety and sophistication that good legal analysis demands at the same time.

For the Defense of the Themselves and the State is not a breezy read like *Stopping Power*. It is 274 pages of single-spaced, small (but readable) text. This is a serious book.

Any lawyer or historian with an interest in the right to arms will find the book fascinating. The book would be an excellent donation to a college library or a law school library. It would also do fine at a public library or a high school library.

Although Cramer is only a graduate student, he has written a more substantial book than at least 75% of all professors will ever produce. (About half of all tenured professors never write a single book.) Cramer's execution of such an important piece of research and synthesis so early in his scholarly career suggests that over the coming decades, people interested in the gun issue will be reading quite a lot of Clayton Cramer's words.

God and Guns

One of the most annoying features of the current gun control debate is the self-righteous attitude of so many of the gun banners. Initially, the self-righteous attitude seems surprising, since the gun prohibitionists couch their arguments in non-moral, pragmatic terms. (i.e. "a gun in the home is more likely to endanger someone in your family than to protect you.") Gun-owners, of course, shoot back their own pragmatic arguments. (i.e. "in the hands of non-alcoholic, non-felon owners, guns are much more likely to be used for protection than to be used against an innocent person.")

Neither side of this pragmatic argument would seem to have a lock on morality; both sides want to protect innocent life. The two sides just have different views about the practical consequences of various self-protection strategies.

So why then, do the antis so often assume an air of high moral superiority? Because a great many of the gun prohibitionists believe that the use of force, especially deadly force, by anybody other than the government is immoral. In stamping out guns, they are stamping out the "immoral" desire to use deadly force to protect oneself or one's family. The anti-gun moralists (who, intolerantly, want to impose their morality on everybody else) often claim that their mandated pacifism is the proper Christian ethic.

Not. Two religious scholars—Brendan F.J. Furnish and Dwight H. Small—confront the issue head-on in their book *The Mounting Threat of Home Intruders: Weighing the Moral Option of Self-Defense*. (Published by the Charles C. Thomas company in Springfield, Illinois, the book is 257 pages long, and sells for $59.95, hardback only.)

Part One of the book provides evidence about the growing threat of violent criminals. Part Three offers the authors' suggestions for an effective firearms policy. (They make a good argument for a "smart card" to be used as identification for gun purchases.) But the most important (and the longest) part of the book is the middle part, titled "Moral and Religious Grounds for Self-Defense." The authors start with the Old Testament, then work their way through the New Testament, and into modern theological ethics.

Carefully considering all contrary arguments, the authors come to the solidly-reasoned conclusion that (within the Judeo-Christian framework) there is no valid basis for denying the right to use deadly force against a violent predator. The "moral" assertion of the gun prohibitionists that use of deadly force against criminals is always wrong is intellectually insupportable. It has no genuine basis in Judeo-Christian ethics.

Furnish and Small treat the anti-force argument respectfully, and their discussion may prove convincing to pacifists who are willing to read the book with an open mind.

In their desire to treat the pacifist position gently, Furnish and Small do not take us to the conclusion which much of their reasoning implies: not only is the use of force in some circumstances a legitimate moral choice, the failure to use force may itself be *immoral*. In other words, if a murderer breaks into your home, and you have the opportunity to shoot him, but you instead let him murder your spouse and children, you have acted in a profoundly immoral manner.

The Mounting Threat of Home Intruders, besides being a good analysis of a particular ethical issue, also serves as an introduction to modern scholarly theology (including the work of the great theologian Reinhold Niebuhr).

Folks who aren't interested in Judeo-Christian ethics will have no use for this book; but folks who want to take issue with the claim of some gun control lobbyists that the only moral choice for crime victims is not to fight back will find this book fascinating.

Besides making a fine donation to public, high school, and college libraries, *The Mounting Threat of Home Intruders* is also a good gift for your favorite high-school student who is attending a religious school, and tussling with teachers who expound the simplistic pacifist line. As Pope John Paul II wrote in a May 3, 1983 Pastoral letter which is quoted in the Furnish/Small book, "...people have a right and even a duty to protect their existence and freedom by proportionate means against an unjust aggressor....Faced with the fact of attack on the innocent, the presumption that we do no harm, even to our enemy, yields to the command of love understood as the need to restrain an enemy who would injure the innocent."

Guns, Crime and Freedom
(Review first printed in *American Rifleman*)

With our Second Amendment rights under constant assault by a President preoccupied with imagery, a media with little interest in the truth, and gun prohibition lobbies which are as brilliant at hate-mongering and disinformation as they are contemptuous of the Constitution, it's no wonder that gun-owners sometimes feel besieged.

As fast as you can learn the real facts about one issue (such as so-called "assault weapons"), the gun prohibition lobby ventriloquists and their media/political dummies are spouting a new line of nonsense (such as gun buy-backs). Where can you find a single resource that will refute all the diverse threads of gun control propaganda, a resource that puts together the whole puzzle of the gun rights battle? The place to go is your local bookstore for a copy of Wayne LaPierre's new book *Guns, Crime, and Freedom.* (Published by Regnery, with a foreword by Tom Clancy).

All of the gun control issues that have dominated the headlines are discussed, chapter by chapter. From waiting periods to "treating guns like cars" to children and guns, it's all there.

Particularly important is the chapter discussing the upcoming agenda of the gun prohibition lobbies and President Clinton. They have already announced plans to turn you into a felon for owning two bricks of .22 ammo without a license, to make you get permission from the government simply to retain the guns you already own, and to tax ammunition so heavily that target practice will be feasible only for the wealthy.

And happily, you'll also find chapters about how Americans all across the nation are rejecting the claims of the gun prohibition lobbies that ordinary people are too stupid, unstable, and clumsy to own guns for self-defense. As government fails to protect the people, the people, in record numbers, are choosing to protect themselves and their families.

Particularly heartening in this regard is LaPierre's chapter on concealed carry reform, detailing how the NRA has helped win laws all over the country guaranteeing the right of good citizens to carry handguns for protection.

No matter how well you know the gun issue, you will find valuable new information. You'll learn the truth about the real Oskar Schindler, hero of the award-winning movie *Schindler's List*. Towards the end of World War II, Schindler obtained Gewehr 41 W's (a German semi-automatic military rifle) and gave them to his Jewish workers, so they could resist the Nazis. That part of the real story, of course, never made it into the politically correct Hollywood version.

Whether you are veteran gun rights activist or a fresh recruit in the battle to defend the Second Amendment, you'll find *Guns, Crime, and Freedom* to be an important resource for educating yourself and others. The book is an excellent gift for your friends who are interested in a good introduction to the gun rights issue. It is also a good reference book for your letters to the editor, communications with elected officials, and other public education efforts.

As NRA members, we have been subject to an unceasing hate campaign by certain politicians and the media for not being "reasonable" and surrendering a portion of our rights by giving in to whatever happens to be at the top of the gun prohibition lobbies' agenda. Besides demolishing the particular items on the gun-banners' agenda, LaPierre also explains why the NRA doesn't back down on the Second Amendment: because you can't compromise with Constitutional rights, and because appeasement of the gun prohibitionists simply produces new demands for the surrender of more rights.

One of the best things about the book is what *isn't* in it: hunting and target shooting. This doesn't mean that those topics are unimportant to LaPierre (who is a hunter) or to the NRA (which won several major pro-hunting votes in the 103rd Congress). But what the Second Amendment is fundamentally about is not sports, but about the right to defend oneself against criminals, including criminals who may run a government. As the book's title indicates, the right to bear arms is ultimately the right to be free.

The book isn't perfect, however. The index is weak; for example, there's no entry for "Schindler's List."

And LaPierre has apparently been spending most of his evenings at work rather than watching MTV or NBA basketball, since he calls Michael Jackson a basketball star. (He meant Michael Jordan.)

About a quarter of the book is devoted to LaPierre's ideas for strengthening the criminal justice system. Many of the crime-fighting provisions are sensible, and long overdue. For example, LaPierre calls for greater victim's rights, including the right to be informed if the criminal is released from prison, or if he escapes.

Likewise, LaPierre argues that criminals should be barred from suing for injuries they suffer while perpetrating or fleeing from a crime. This reform would put an end to the ridiculous cases like the one where a burglar sued (successfully!) a building owner because the burglar was climbing on a roof and fell through a skylight that had been painted black.

But some of LaPierre's other suggestions (such as allowing people to sentenced for using a gun in a crime even when the prosecution has not proven beyond a reasonable doubt that a gun was actually used) threaten to weaken traditional American civil liberties. As we vigorously demand full enforcement of the Second Amendment, we cannot be less protective of the rest of the Bill of Rights, including the provisions that apply to persons accused or convicted of crimes.

We should also remember that (thanks to the bigots at the gun prohibition lobbies), millions of decent people in places like California, New Jersey, and Connecticut have been turned into "gun criminals." Can we be sure that new governmental powers created to fight violent crime will not one day be turned against good citizens who violate gun prohibition laws?

Guns, Crime, and Freedom explains why Wayne LaPierre has devoted his life to defending the Second Amendment against attacks by forces who believe that the government should be strong and the people weak. While the book is full of information, what keeps the book moving is LaPierre's passion for freedom. If you share that passion, this book will help you defend our sacred freedoms. And if you don't yet share that passion, this book may help you develop one.

English History

Almost as long as Americans have been discussing guns and government restrictions on guns, they have been looking to the example set by Great Britain; and almost without exception, they have misunderstood the legal and social reality of gun control in Great Britain. Historian Joyce Lee Malcolm's book, *To Keep and Bear Arms: The Origins of an Anglo-American Right* does much to correct the confused American mind. In particular, the book gives special attention to the latter half of the 17th century in Britain, a period of internal turmoil and repression that culminated in the adoption of a British Bill of Rights, which included an explicit right to arms. This document laid the foundations for the American Bill of Rights and, specifically, the Second Amendment. This is an excellent book of legal history, which illuminates the timeless struggle between liberty and tyranny. (Cambridge, Mass.: Harvard University Press. 1994).

Lethal Laws

Genocide is a human rights violation that dwarves all the rest. If we are to be about human rights, then we must be serious about eradicating genocide. By studying the gun control laws of eight countries which perpetrated genocide in the twentieth century (Turkey, Germany, USSR, China, Uganda, Cambodia, Guatemala) Jay Simkin, Aaron Zelman, and Alan M. Rice have shown that a well-armed population which is prepared to resist is much less likely to be murdered by its government than a disarmed population. Their book *Lethal* Laws demonstrates that if the people of the world were much better armed, many fewer people would be the victims of genocide. The book is published by Jews for the Preservation of Firearms Ownership, Inc., 2872 South Wentworth Avenue, Milwaukee, WI 53207, (414) 769-0760.

Shall Issue: The New Wave of Concealed Handgun Permits Laws

This is a ninety page report that Dave Kopel co-wrote with Clayton Cramer. The report examines all the available evidence regarding state laws which mandate that trained citizens who pass a background check cannot be arbitrarily denied a permit to carry a concealed handgun for protection. The report concludes that concealed carry laws *may* reduce violent crime, and certainly do not cause additional problems for law enforcement. The report is available for twelve dollars from: Independence Institute, 14142 Denver West Parkway, Suite 185, Golden, Colo. 80401 (303) 279-6536.

Guns: Who Should Have Them?

This book, slated for publication in the summer of 1995, covers a variety of gun control topics. Feminist scholar Mary Zeiss Stange examines the question of women and guns. Robert Cottrol and Ray Diamond dissect how gun control has historically been used to disarm African-Americans. Don Kates and two co-authors debunk the "public health" propaganda in favor of gun control. Finally, Dave Kopel supplies three chapters: on waiting periods, "assault weapons," and children and guns. The book will be available in many bookstores, or directly from Prometheus Books (Amherst, N.Y.).

Gun Control and the Constitution

Edited by law professor Robert Cottrol, this one-volume anthology collects the most important legal documents related to the Second Amendment. Included in the book are three court cases and ten major law review articles. Cottrol is scrupulously fair about presenting law reviews from both sides of the gun issue, but if you read all ten articles, you won't have much doubt about whether the Second Amendment guarantees an individual right. *Gun Control and the Constitution* is available from Garland Publishing, (800) 627-6273, and sells for $18.95, paperback.

Point Blank

Our previous book, *Things You Can Do to Defend Your Gun Rights*, contained a lengthy review of Gary Kleck's book, *Point Blank*, which is the single best source of research regarding guns and gun control ever published. A new edition of the book is coming out in paperback, so there will be no excuse for not adding this book to your collection!

Defender Database

This is a DOS computer program containing all items from the American Rifleman's "Armed Citizen" column. It's very straightforward and easy to use. For more information, contact: A. Chatzithhomas, 202B Crystal Brook Hollow Rd., Port Jefferson Station, NY, 11776.

Still More Books

Besides the above books about firearms, here are some other important books analyzing the theory and practice of freedom:

Aristotle, Numerous works. It's only a slight exaggeration to say that the current gun control debate continues the debate between Plato (favoring a totalitarian state, ruled by an elite) and Aristotle (favoring self-rule) that started long ago in the groves of Ancient Greece. Read for yourself what one of the seminal thinkers of human freedom and natural law has to say.

Bruce Benson, *The Enterprise of Law* (S.F.: Pacific Research Institute, 1990). A brilliant historical and imaginative book which explains how societies have had law without needing a government—and how America can build such a society in the future.

John Locke, *Two Treatises on Government*. One of the founding documents for a political theory of property rights, natural law, and limited government. Perhaps the greatest pro-freedom work of political philosophy of all time.

John Stuart Mill, *On Liberty* (1859). An easily-readable, short book which articulates the great principle of modern liberty: "The only purpose for which power can rightfully be exercised over any member of a civilized community, against his will, is to prevent harm to others...Over himself, over his own body and mind, the individual is sovereign."

Some other great works that you'll profit from: Frederic Bastiat, *The Law*; Clint Bolick, *Grass-Roots Tyranny*; James Bovard, *Lost* Rights; Milton Friedman, *Free to* Choose; F.A. Hayek, *The Road to Serfdom, Our Enemy the State, The Constitution of Liberty*; Thomas Jefferson, *The Declaration of Independence*; Ken Kesey, *One Flew Over the Cuckoo's Nest*; Madeleine L'Engle, *A Wrinkle in Time*; Charles Mackay, *Extraordinary Popular Delusions and the Madness of Crowds*; Baron de Montesquieu, *The Spirit of the Laws*; John Milton, *Areopagitica*; Robert Nozick, *Anarchy, State, and Utopia*; P.J. O'Rourke, *Parliament of Whores*; George Orwell, *1984*; Thomas Paine, *Common Sense, The Rights of Man*; Sheldon Richman, *Separating School and State*; Adam Smith, *The Wealth of Nations*; Sophocles, *Antigone*; Lysander Spooner, *An Essay on the Trial by Jury*.

Many of these books, and plenty of other good ones, can be obtained from Laissez Faire Books, 938 Howard St. #202, San Francisco, CA 94103. (800) 326-0996.

Magazines

Here are some good pro-freedom magazines that you'll enjoy:

Claustrophobia. Very funny monthly newsletter, with a libertarian slant. Issues average about 12 pages. Subscriptions are $10 per year, from Claustrophobia, 400 North High St., #137, Columbus, OH 43215. (614) 444-6561. E-mail: phobia@bronze.coil.com.

Reason. The leading pro-freedom magazine in the United States. A superb monthly featuring the best libertarian writers. In contrast to many political magazines, *Reason* often uses writers with a high degree of scientific expertise. Subscriptions are $19.95 per year. 3415 S. Sepulveda Blvd., Suite 400, Los Angeles, CA 90034. (800) 998-8989.

The Right Mind. A very funny conservative/libertarian monthly newsletter. Send a check for $20 for twelve issues to Conservative SIG, PO Box 2047, Carmichael, CA 95609.

Washington Times, Weekly Edition. Learn plenty of Washington inside gossip, from a newspaper that is just as partisan as the *Washington Post*, but much better at reporting. These are the folks who uncovered the Whitewater scandal. A six-month subscription costs $34.95; a two year subscription $79.95. (800) 636-3679.

14. Videos

> "THOSE WHO SAY THAT LIFE IS WORTH LIVING AT ANY COST HAVE ALREADY WRITTEN FOR THEMSELVES AN EPITAPH OF INFAMY, FOR THERE IS NO CAUSE AND NO PERSON THAT THEY WILL NOT BETRAY TO STAY ALIVE."
>
> —Sidney Hook.

These videos can provide you with entertaining information about current gun rights issues. The videos are also a good way to educate your friends. You can invite them over to watch the video with you, or you can loan them the video after you watch it.

Videos are great for gun club meetings. They can also be set up in gun stores (or on tables at gun shows). They're a good way to get customers to stay in the store, or to spend some time at your gun show table.

Most electronics stores now have "all-in-one" machines that combine a television with a built-in VCR. These machines are often designed for portability.

National Rifle Association videos

An increasing number of cable television systems are now carrying the National Empowerment Television channel. This channel provides 24 hours a day of conservative political and family-oriented programming. Included in the NET programming is an hour-long show produced by the NRA, titled "On Target." Programs deal with topics such as "Is Gun Control a Public Health Issue?" and "Victims: Survivors of Violent Crime Speak Out."

If you don't receive NET on your cable system, you can order tapes of each program for $14.95 (or six episodes for $59.95), plus three dollars shipping and handling per tape. To order, contact the NRA/ILA Fiscal Office.

The NRA also produces a monthly video Report from Washington for activists. You can arrange to receive these by contracting the NRA Grassroots Office. (The main NRA number is 703-267-1000.)

Gun Owners of America videotapes

This small but feisty gun rights group has a number of excellent videotapes, including:

The Assault on Semi-Automatic Firearms. (28 minutes). An expose of the most serious attack on our right to bear arms since the days of King George III.

Breaking the Law in the Name of the Law. (40 minutes). Victims of abuses (including some police officers) by the Bureau of Alcohol, Tobacco and Firearms speak out.

When BATF sent an "undercover" agent into the Branch Davidian compound in Waco, Texas, the Davidians knew that he was spying on them. Nevertheless, Branch Davidian leader David Koresh attempted to befriend him, and to convert him to Branch Davidian religion. Koresh also showed the BATF agent a copy of this tape documenting the BATF's criminal record.

The agent almost switched sides, and joined the Branch Davidians.

This powerful tape probably won't make you want to become Branch Davidian. But it will help you learn what a menace to law-abiding citizens the Bureau of Alcohol, Tobacco and Firearms has become.

Jacquie Miller Speaks Out. The gun prohibitionists love gun crime victims. Except when the victims don't go along with the gun-banning agenda.

In 1989, a nut named Joseph Wesbecker, inspired by *Time* magazine's lurid coverage of Stockton school yard massacre, began shooting people at a Louisville, Kentucky printing plant. One of the plant's employees, Jacquie Miller, ran to her office to grab her handgun. She was seconds from drawing her gun and stopping Wesbecker when he shot her in the back. She is now confined to a wheelchair.

When Jacquie Miller attempted to testify about her experience before the United States House of Representatives Subcommittee on Crime, Subcommittee Chairman Charles Schumer wouldn't let her, once he found out that she opposed gun control.

She went to the hearing anyway, and sat in the front row. Schumer ordered the security guards to rearrange the chairs, so that television cameras wouldn't be able to see Jacquie Miller.

Shortly afterward, a television journalist asked Schumer why he wouldn't let Jacquie Miller testify. Schumer claimed that Miller has testified before Congress before, and he only wanted to hear new witnesses. The statement was completely false; Miller had never testified before.

The Jacquie Miller video tells the compelling story of a gun crime victim who believes more firmly than ever in defending her Constitutional rights. The video tells you the story that Charles Schumer tried to hide from the American people.

The Truth About AK-47 Power. Larry Pratt (Director of Gun Owners of America) and Neal Knox (an NRA leader, and a national shooting champion) demolish the fraud that "assault weapons" are more powerful than other guns. Pratt and Knox shoot watermelons with a Kalashnikov rifle, an M-10 "assault pistol," an old-fashioned hunting rifle, and a 12 gauge shotgun. Guess which weapons make the watermelons crack, and which weapons blast the watermelons to smithereens?

All of the Gun Owners of America videos can be ordered by calling (800) 552-9944.

Part III

Firearms Business and Activity

For decades, most of the American gun business lazily sat on the sidelines, while the NRA, CCRKBA, and other consumer groups did the hard work of defending the Second Amendment. Finally, many folks in the gun business are starting to realize that if they don't start defending their rights, they're going to be out of business pretty soon.

If you run a gun store, it's your obligation to make your store a focal point of Second Amendment activism. And if you buy firearms products, it is your obligation to buy products from companies that actively support your rights.

15. Run a Pro-Gun Gun Store

> "EXPERIENCE SHOULD TEACH US TO BE MOST ON OUR GUARD TO PROTECT LIBERTY WHEN THE GOVERNMENT'S PURPOSES ARE BENEFICENT. MEN BORN TO FREEDOM ARE NATURALLY ALERT TO REPEL INVASION OF THEIR LIBERTY BY EVIL-MINDED RULERS. THE GREATEST DANGERS TO LIBERTY LURK IN INSIDIOUS ENCROACHMENT BY MEN OF ZEAL, WELL MEANING BUT WITHOUT UNDERSTANDING."
>
> —Supreme Court Justice Louis Brandeis, *Olmstead* v. *United States*, 277 U.S. 438 (1928).

Browsing in a gun store is often a depressing experience for us. True, there are interesting guns and accessories to look at, but well over half of all gun stores do absolutely nothing to inform their customers about what is going on with the Second Amendment. Too many stores make zero effort to energize and mobilize their customers to fight for freedom. There are so many easy ways for stores to get into the political arena, it's disgraceful how few of them do. Stores which stand on the sidelines of the Second Amendment struggle don't earn a second visit from us, nor should they from any other pro-rights gun owner.

In contrast, stores that care enough about their long-term future to help insure the availability of firearms to ordinary Americans twenty years from now are also the stores which tend to be most knowledgeable about guns, and to give the best customer service. Here are some ways you can your gun store into a freedom center:

★ Keep a supply of pro-gun leaflets and pamphlets at the counter.

★ Keep a supply of voting registration information at the counter. If your state allows it, register you customers to vote on the spot.

★ Display window signs for pro-gun candidates at election time.

★ Ask a local pro-rights group to set up a table outside

your store on a busy weekend day.

★ Advertise in gun rights publications. Newsletters of state and local rights groups are particularly hungry for advertising. It's a low-cost way to reach a core of highly motivated gun owners.

★ Encourage customers to join the NRA or CCRKBA or SAF. Make it easy for them to join by having sign-up material on hand at the counter.

The National Rifle Association has a special dealer program, which allows stores to keep some of the revenue generated from signing up new NRA members. Contact the NRA Membership Division, and ask for the manager of Dealer Programs. (703-267-1000). The NRA has a large supply of promotional materials they can send you, to encourage sign-ups.

In conjunction with signing up members for the NRA (or a different gun group if you prefer) give a 5% discount to NRA members, or persons carrying a membership card from another pro-rights group.

When ringing up a purchase, ask a customer if he belongs to the NRA, and if he doesn't, ask if you can put information about how to join in his sack.

For customers who make purchases over a certain amount, buy a membership for the customer.

Put a glass jar on your check-out counter, with a pro-gun bumper sticker. Cut a slit in the lid on the top, so that people can drop in contributions of one, five, ten, or twenty dollars to the pro-rights cause. Then send the money you collect you your favorite gun-rights group.

A more formal version of the glass jar with a lid is the NRA Round-Up program, by which your customers can round their purchases up to the next dollar, and donate the spare change to the NRA Foundation or the NRA Endowment to Protect the Second Amendment. Alternatively, or additionally, customers can contribute by putting their spare change into a countertop Round-Up display. The countertop display includes a flyer which the NRA updates every three months.

Finally, you can make regular, tax-deductible contributions to the NRA Foundation (discussed in chapter 5), as part of the NRA Foundation Fair Share program, designed especially for gun stores. For information on these NRA programs, call the NRA Development Office at (703) 267-1129.

Also at your front counter, set up a supply of postcards pre-addressed to your Congress people and Governor. Encourage customers to write a short message expressing support for the right to keep and bear arms; customers should include their address so the elected official can write back. You can take care of stamping and mailing the cards.

Firearms Dealers Association

If your state has an association of licensed firearms dealers, join it. If your state doesn't, then form one! To find out how a dealer's association can play a constructive, pro-freedom role in state gun policy debates, contact the Sanford Abrams, vice-president of the Maryland Licensed Firearms Dealers Association, PO Box 2555, Silver Spring, MD 20915-2555. (301) 942-3329; fax (301) 942-7946.

Customers

At your gun store, look for pro-rights literature. Does the store encourage customers to join the NRA or other pro-rights groups? To take safety classes? Does the store donate a specified percentage of profits to pro-gun causes?

If the gun store doesn't have any pro-rights literature, ask them if they would display NRA literature if you brought it in. If they say no, take your business to a pro-gun gun store. If they say yes, order a pack of NRA brochures from the NRA's Institute for Legislative Action. (As we discussed in our first book, *Things You Can Do to Defend Your Gun Rights*, NRA has large supplies of free brochures available for public education.)

16. Gun Shows

"I DO BELIEVE THAT WHERE THERE IS A CHOICE ONLY BETWEEN COWARDICE AND VIOLENCE, I WOULD ADVISE VIOLENCE. THUS WHEN MY ELDEST SON ASKED ME WHAT HE SHOULD HAVE DONE HAD HE BEEN PRESENT WHEN I WAS ALMOST FATALLY ASSAULTED IN 1908, WHETHER HE SHOULD HAVE RUN AWAY AND SEEN ME KILLED OR WHETHER HE SHOULD HAVE USED HIS PHYSICAL FORCE WHICH COULD AND WANTED TO USE, AND DEFEND ME, I TOLD HIM IT WAS HIS DUTY TO DEFEND ME EVEN BY USING VIOLENCE."
—Mohandas K. Gandhi, "Young India," Aug. 11, 1920, quoted in Louis Fischer (editor) *The Essential Gandhi*, pp. 156-57.

If you put on gun shows, then make sure to become a member of the National Association of Gun Shows, which is directed by the Citizens Committee for the Right to Keep and Bear Arms, 12500 NE Tenth Place, Bellevue, WA 98005. (206) 454-4911. NAGS provides gun show organizers with grassroots educational materials, displays, and other tools to help get gun show customers politically activated.

The "Beinfeld Initiative," invented by Las Vegas gun show promoter Wallace Beinfeld offers an important way to make gun shows into pro-gun revenue raisers. At Beinfeld's gun shows, he charges exhibitors an extra two dollars a table. He matches the two dollars with two dollars of his own, and then sends the extra four dollars (per table) to the NRA's Institute for Legislative Action. Beinfeld also raised the customer admission price from $4.50 to $5.00, and gives the extra 50 cents to ILA too.

Stores and ranges could try similar initiatives. A range, for example, could raise its fee by 50 cents, and send the money to a pro-gun organization. A store could offer customers a matching gift program; if the customer contributes five or ten dollars on the spot to a pro-gun group, the store will match the contribution.

17. Buy Guns and Accessories from
Pro-gun Companies

"CERTAINLY ONE OF THE CHIEF GUARANTEES OF FREEDOM UN-
DER ANY GOVERNMENT, NO MATTER HOW POPULAR AND RE-
SPECTED, IS THE RIGHT OF CITIZENS TO KEEP AND BEAR
ARMS...THE RIGHT OF CITIZENS TO BEAR ARMS IS JUST ONE GUAR-
ANTEE AGAINST ARBITRARY GOVERNMENT, ONE MORE SAFEGUARD
AGAINST THE TYRANNY WHICH NOW APPEARS REMOTE IN AMERICA
BUT WHICH HISTORICALLY HAS PROVEN TO BE ALWAYS POSSIBLE."
—Sen. Hubert H. Humphrey (1960).

If a company that sells firearms or firearms-related products is too selfish to help defend your rights, they don't deserve
your business, whether you're a consumer or a gun store. Here's
a list of some of the companies which have gone the extra mile in
defending gun rights.

Gun Manufacturers
    Calico Light Weapons. Among other good works, Calico
is a strong supporter of Jews for the Preservation of Firearms
Ownership.
    Colt's Manufacturing Co. When Colt's vice-president
testified against a semi-automatic ban before the U.S. House Judiciary Committee in 1991, it was the first time in over half a
century that a gun company executive had testified before Congress against gun control. Colt's executives spend lots of time on
Capitol Hill lobbying against gun prohibition. Colt's employees
sent over 1,000 letters to Congress to support gun rights.
    European American Armory. This handgun company
ran a "Fight for Freedom" promotion which provided NRA membership applications with every firearm sold. Buyers also received
complimentary subscriptions to the American Shooting Sports
Council's newsletter.
    Heckler & Koch. H&K's President CEO Florian Deltgen
sent letters to other gun companies urging them to offer financial

support to a pro-gun candidate in a crucial State Senate race in H&K's home state of Virginia.

O. F. Mossberg & Sons, Inc. Mossberg vice-president and General Counsel Georgia Nichols has emerged as one of the industry's most tireless spokespersons, flying all over the United States to meet with public officials and defend the Second Amendment. Mossberg is a strong supporter of the pro-rights American Shooting Sports Coalition. Contrary to rumor, Mossberg does *not* support any laws requiring guns to be stored locked. Mossberg does, however, have an excellent program making trigger locks available with every gun it sells.

Springfield Armory has published an excellent brochure called "What do you tell them when they ask 'Why does anyone need military style guns?'" S.A.'s Raymond Pilgrim has lobbied hard in Congress against gun bans.

Springfield Armory also sponsors a huge number of shooting competitions.

Ammunition and Reloading Companies

Dillon Precision Products. The Scottsdale, Arizona manufacturer of reloading equipment pays part of the first-year NRA membership fee for its customers. Dillon's catalog, *The Blue Press*, reserves plenty of space for pro-gun articles. (In fact, Dave writes a regular column for them.) To get on the mailing list for the free monthly catalogue, call (800) 421-7632, or (602) 948-8009.

Hansen Cartridge Co. Southport, Connecticut. The company's President, Jay Hansen, is a strong supporter of the American Shooting Sports Council (more on them below).

Midway. This reloading company invented "Operation NRA Round-Up." Every customer is asked if they would like to "round up" their order to the nearest dollar. Once a month, Midway sends the round up money to the NRA Institute for Legislative Action, and throws in an additional $1,000 check from Midway itself. In 1994, Midway raised a fantastic $303,183.50 for NRA.

Accessory Companies

Conetrol Scope Mounts. Conetrol initiated "The NRA Percent" program. Every customer who shows an NRA membership card gets a 1% discount. The discount is also available to dealers and wholesalers who offer the NRA Percent to their customers; participating companies receive a 12" by 5" decal suitable for display.

Says Conetrol: "Let us all work toward the day when a customer in any sporting goods store in the country will be asked at the close of every transaction involving a hunting or shooting product: 'Are you a member of the National Rifle Association?'"

When you buy shooting or hunting goods, ask your dealer if he participates in the NRA Percent program. If he doesn't, let him know about Conetrol's program, and urge that he do so.

Muzzle-Nuzzle. These folks make excellent woven storage covers for firearms. The "muzzle nuzzle" is a very good device for protecting high-quality firearms stored in your gun safe, and a very important device for firearms that have to be put into long-term, perhaps hidden, storage. Muzzle-Nuzzle sells a booklet called *Cache Tips*, which details the mechanics of the long-term hiding of a firearm. The booklet sells for three dollars, which is well below the production cost; the book may only be purchased in conjunction with another Muzzle-Nuzzle product.

Ram-Line. A producer of plastic magazines and other after market components, they also make a partly plastic .22 pistol. They played a major role in working to defeat the "assault weapons" ban in Colorado.

Distributors

Gander Mountain. These Wisconsin folks run a mail-order catalog for hunting and outdoor goods. When the city of Wilmot, Wisconsin had referendum on banning the possession of handguns, Gander stepped into action. Gander organized its employees and those of other companies into a phone bank which called pro-gun voters and urged them to get out and vote. Thanks to Gander's efforts, the gun ban was defeated by a margin of 2-1.

RSR Wholesale Guns. Senior vice-president and Corporate Counsel, Mike Saporito has testified against semi-auto bans. He also served as Chair of the State of Florida's Commission on "Assault Weapons," winning praise from all sides for his fair-minded approach to his duties, as well as for educating the public and defusing hysteria. In 1991, RSR was a co-winner of the "Industry Minuteman Award" given by the Citizens Committee for the Right to Keep and Bear Arms.

More recently, Mike has set up "Mike's Militia" to provide gun dealers with fax reports about gun control legislation. These faxes can then be photocopied, and distributed to customers.

Delta Press. This mail-order catalogue of gun-related books gives the NRA's telephone number in every catalogue, and encourages readers to join.

American Shooting Sports Council

One way to find out if a manufacturer or other company is active in the gun rights movement is to see if they belong to the American Shooting Sports Coalition. This industry organization was founded in 1989 in response to some of the biggest gun products manufacturers deciding to throw most of our gun rights to the wolves. Members of the ASSC are proud to be "As Pro-Gun As Our Customers."

Conversely, companies that refuse to join the ASSC may be companies that put little practical effort into defending our rights. Among the companies that have refused to help ASSC are the Federal Cartridge Co. And Ruger.

Below is a list of ASSC members, as of December 19, 1994:

Wholesalers

Acusport Corporation; AJ Wholesale Gun Distributors, Inc.; Alamo Leather Goods, Inc.; Amchar Wholesale, Inc.; Ashland Shooting Supply; Automatic Distributing Corporation; Bangers L.P.; Baxter South Inc.; Brazas Sporting Arms, Inc.; Bumble Bee

Wholesale; Conevera's Guns, Inc.; Davidson's; Eagle Exim, Inc.; Ellett Brothers; Fox Wholesale, Inc.; GO/Sportsmen's Supply, Inc.; Graf & Sons; Gunarama Wholesale; Hill Country Wholesale, Inc.; Jack First, Inc.; J & S Wholesale; Kiesler Police Supply, Inc.; Lew Horton Distributing Co.; Lipsey's Inc.; L.M. Burney, Inc.; Maurice Sporting Goods, Inc.; Micro Sight Company; Nationwide Sports Distributors; P & B Enterprises; Point Sporting Goods; RSR Wholesale Guns, Inc.; Schaub Distributors; Scott's Inc.; Scott Wholesale Co., Inc.; SG Distributing; Sports South, Inc.; Southern Ohio Gun Distributors, Inc.; Western Hoegee Company.; W.L. Baumler Company.

Member-owned Distributor
Sports, Inc.

Manufacturers & Importers
Action Arms, Ltd.; Adco International; American Ammunition; American Arms; Arcadia Machine & Tool, Inc.; Auto Ordnance Corporation; B-square Company; B-West Imports, Inc.; Bagmaster Manufacturing, Inc.; Barnes Bullets Inc.; Beretta U.S.A. Corporation; Bianchi International; Black Hills Ammunition, Inc.; Boonie Packer Prods./JFS, Inc.; Buffalo Bullet Co., Inc.; Bushmaster Firearms; Butler Creek Corporation; Break-Free, Inc.; Calico Light Weapon Systems; Charco, Inc.; Colt Blackpowder Arms Company; Colt's Manufacturing Co.; Crosman Corporation; Davis Industries; Dynamit Nobel RWS, Inc.; Eagle Arms, Inc.; Eagle Imports, Inc.; Eagle International, Inc.; European American Armory; Feather Industries, Inc.; Fratelli Tanfoglio S.R.L.; Galco International, Ltd.; Glaser Safety Slug, Inc.; Glock, Inc.; Goex, Inc. ; Gun Parts Corporation; Gun Vault, Inc.; H & R 1871, Inc.; Hansen Cartridge Company; Heckler & Koch; Heritage Manufacturing, Inc.; Hide-a-gun ; High Standard Manufacturing Co., Inc.; Hodgdon Powder Company; Hogue Inc.; Hornady Manufacturing Company; Huntington Die Specialties; IMI Services USA; Interarms; Intrac Corporation; Intratec; J & J Products; K-Sports Imports, Inc.; K.B.I., Inc.; Keng's Firearms Spe-

cialty, Inc.; Kleen-Bore, Inc.; Knight's Manufacturing Company; Laser Devices, Inc.; Liberty Arms Works, Inc.; Lorcin Engineering Company; Magnum Research, Inc.; Marlin Firearms Company; Mayville Engineering Co.; Mec-gar USA, Inc.; Michaels of Oregon; Millett Industries; MTM Molded Products Co.; North American Arms; Nosler, Inc.; O.F. Mossberg & Sons; Olin/Winchester Corporation; Olympic Arms; Ox-yoke Originals, Inc.; Pachmayr Ltd.; Para-ordnance Mfg., Inc.; Phoenix Arms; Precision Small Arms, Inc.; Ram-line, Inc.; Redfield, Inc.; Remington Arms Company, Inc.; Savage Arms, Inc.; Sightron, Inc.; Silencio/safety Direct Co.; Smith & Wesson; Speedfeed, Inc.; Springfield, Inc.; Stoeger Industries; Sundance Industries, Inc.; Tasco Sales, Inc.; Taurus International, Inc.; 3-D Ammo and Bullets; Trijicon, Inc.; Tru-fire Corporation; U.S.A. Magazines, Inc.; Washington Trading Company, Inc.; Wesson Firearms Co., Inc.; Zero Ammunition Co., Inc.

Retailers

Ace Sporting Goods; Armament Gunsmithing Co., Inc.; B & R Guns Outdoor Range, Inc.; Badger Guns & Ammo, Inc.; Beverly Hills Gun Shop; Bighorn Trading Co.; Blue Lakes Sporting Goods, Inc.; Big City Pawn; Big River Sports; Brady's Sportsman Supplies; Brinkman Bookkeeping, Inc.; Buck's Gun Rack; Burlington Pawnbrokers; C. Discount Guns; Cabela's Inc.; Capital Sports & Western Wear; Caso's Gun-a-rama Inc.; Chuck's Dolton Gun Shop; Chuck's Gun and Pawn; Continental Guns; Country General Stores; Custom Gun Works; D & R Sports Center; Dan's Gun Repair; Dashiell's Half-round Showroom; Dean's Sporting Goods; Degoff's Firearms, Inc.; Dick's Gun Room, Inc.; Don's Store; Duncan's Gun Shop; Dunkelberger's Sports Outfitter; Dunn's Discount Guns & Sporting Goods, Inc.; Ed's Gun Shop; Fauntleroy Supply, Inc.; Fin & Feather; Firearms Unlimited, Inc.; Frank's Sport Shop; G.A.T. Guns; Guitar's, Inc.; Guns by S.A.M.M.; Guns Galore; Hal's Pawn & Gun Shop; Hart True-Value Hardware & Sporting Goods; Henderson's Sports Ltd.; Jalensky's Sports; Jay's Sporting Goods, Inc.; Jones Gun Shop;

Kent's Sport Store; Kevin Inc.; Kimber of America; Lakes Region Sports, Inc.; Lakeview Hardware Co., Inc.; Laporte Sporting Goods; M & M Sporting Goods Co., Inc.; M.A.C.'s Gun Store, Inc.; Mack's Sport Shop; Mahoney's Sportsman Paradise; Manchester Brothers, Inc.; Mccrea's Gun Shop; Mega Sports; Mel's Trading Post, Inc.; Midwest Sporting Goods; Monsoor's Sport Shop; Mountainside Supply Company, Inc.; Norm's Sports Center; Ohio Valley Trading & Exchange Company; Old Fontenelle Guns; Outfitters Ltd.; Parks Sportsman; Primetime Sports, Inc.; Rancho Gun Shop, Inc.; Reed's Sport Shop, Inc.; Riley's Sport Shop, Inc.; Robertson's; Ronan Sports & Western; Ross' Coin & Gun; S.B. Jeffries Consultants; San Francisco Gun Exchange; Shooter's World; Sioux Sporting Goods; Snappy Sport Senter, Inc.; Southern Maryland Firearms; Southern Trading & Loan, Inc.; Sportsman's Den; Sprague's Sports & R.V., Inc.; Steve's Outdoor Sports & Marine, Inc.; Tactical & Survival Specialties, Inc.; The Gun Trader; The Outdoorsman; The Outdoorsman, Inc.; The Powder Horn; The Sportsman's Gun Shop; Tolan's Gun Shop; Triangle Gun Supply; Turner's Outdoorsman; Turner Sports Bag, Inc.; Uncle Sam's Trading Post; Van Wagenen Finance Company.

Firearms Press

Alliance Voice; American Firearms Industry; D.B.I. Books, Inc.; Firearms Business; Guns & Ammo; Gun Tests; Harris Publications, Inc.; Publishers Development Corporation; Shooting Industry; Shooting Times Magazine; Shooting Sports Retailer; Straight Shooting Department (Fishing Tackle Trade News); Wolfe Publishing Company.

Industry Service Related

Austin Sheridan USA, Inc.; Tim Bailey & Associates; Owen J. Brown & Associates; Timothy A. Bumann, Esq.; Chesnut & Associates; Ferguson-Keller Associates, Inc.; Forbes/Ferry and Associates; Frank Carter Company; Gaines C. Smith Company; David Hardy, Esq.; Henson Sales & Marketing, Inc.; Jones & Company, Inc.; Joseph Chiarello & Co., Inc.; Judd & Associates; James

Monroe Associates, Inc.; Carl T. Rowan, Jr., Esq. (Rowan & Grody); Rosse & Associates, Inc.; Sportco Marketing, Inc.

Associations
Illinois Sporting Goods Association; Maryland Licensed Firearms Dealers Association, Inc.; National Association of Sporting Good Wholesalers; U.S. Practical Shooting Association.

Gunsmiths
Lee Baker; Timothy N. Butler; Thomas Duncan; Robert Rowe; Nevada Wise.

Anti-gun Companies
Even worse than refusing to join the ASSC, however, is being an actively *anti-gun* gun company. In this category is New England Firearms/Harrington & Richardson. In February 1994, the Massachusetts Attorney General held a meeting of other attorneys general and gun manufacturers from New England. At the meeting, James Garrison (representing New England Firearms/H&R) stated "I frankly don't see any purpose for those guns from Czechoslovakia, Russia, or China being imported into the United States."

Garrison went on to state that he had just recently joined the firearms industry, that he had never owned a firearm, and that he did not currently own one. When one of the attorneys general stated that some of the gun controls that they were considering might reduce gun sales, Garrison stated "I don't care if my sales go down."

Fair enough, Mr. Garrison. We sure won't be buying any guns from New England Firearms/Harrington & Richardson.

Magazines
The principle of buying guns from pro-gun companies applies for gun magazines as well. Most over-the-counter magazines for gun hobbyists, such as *Guns & Ammo*, *Gun World* (for which Dave writes a column), *Shotgun News*, and *Shooting Times*,

contain at least one article on gun rights in every issue. A few of the hobby magazines, however, have decided not to spend one cent of their production budget supporting the rights which make their magazine possible. Why take advice about buying or using guns from a publisher who won't do a thing to support your right to own guns?

18. Gun Clubs

"IF YOU WILL NOT FIGHT FOR THE RIGHT WHEN YOU CAN EASILY WIN WITHOUT BLOODSHED, IF YOU WILL NOT FIGHT WHEN VICTORY WILL BE SURE AND NOT SO COSTLY, YOU MAY COME TO THE MOMENT WHEN YOU WILL HAVE TO FIGHT WITH ALL THE ODDS AGAINST YOU AND ONLY A PRECARIOUS CHANCE OF SURVIVAL. THERE MAY BE A WORSE CASE. YOU MAY HAVE TO FIGHT WHEN THERE IS NO CHANCE OF VICTORY, BECAUSE IT IS BETTER TO PERISH THAN TO LIVE AS SLAVES."
—Winston Churchill.

One of the strongest weapons in the right to bear arms arsenal is a gun club. Putting several dozen people together who have a strong personal interest in gun ownership is an advantage that the anti-gun side can't match. There's no such thing as a club of people who get together just to talk about how much they hate guns. (Unless you count the staff meetings at NBC News.) Unfortunately, gun clubs too often remain only a *potential* asset to the freedom cause.

Few people have more to lose from the gun prohibition lobby's schemes than do gun club members. Gun club shooters will suffer the most from exorbitant taxes on ammunition, and proposals to allow unannounced police inspections of the home of any person who owns more than a thousand rounds of ammunition or primers (including rimfire) or ten or more guns.

Now that a ban on so-called "assault weapons" has passed Congress, ammunition taxes and unannounced police searches are at the top of Handgun Control, Inc.'s agenda. Yet too many gun clubs have passively remained on the sidelines of the gun control debate.

Here are some suggestions on how every gun-club can strengthen its clout, and help ensure that 20 years from now, it will still be possible to own guns and choose to belong to a gun club.

Most the tips here apply to gun clubs and all other shooting organizations, such as local chapters of gun rights groups or other grass-roots organizations.

Join NRA

First of all, membership in the National Rifle Association ought to be a requirement for club membership. Somebody who is too cheap to spend $35 a year to help the nation's fastest-growing civil rights organization is not responsible enough to deserve club membership.

Register to Vote

Likewise, every club member should be registered to vote, and at least one club meeting should be devoted to providing voter registration information.

As Yale Law Professor Akhil Reed Amar points out, the authors of the Bill of Rights saw gun ownership, voting, and jury duty not only as individual rights, but also as duties of responsible citizenship. They were right. Registering and voting are part of the obligation to protect the freedom that we owe to the next generation.

Affiliate with NRA and CCRKBA

The club itself should affiliate with the NRA, and can also affiliate with the Citizens Committee for the Right to Keep and Bear Arms (206-454-7012). Club affiliation gives the NRA and CCRKBA a contact point to inform gun owners about developments threatening Second Amendment rights. After the NRA and CCRKBA inform club leadership, the leadership can then inform the membership and take action.

To find about how your club can work with NRA, call NRA field services at 703-267-1343. Once you join, NRA will work with you in all sorts of ways to protect your rights, including defeating anti-gun legislation locally, supporting pro-rights candidates in elections, setting up a "fax tree" to alert club members about legislative activity, and working on voter registration drives.

In addition, the National Shooting Sports Foundation (NSSF) publishes a quarterly newsletter, *Gun Club Advisor*, which contains practical and political tips. Contact NSSF, 11 Mile Hill Road, Newtown, Conn., 06470-2359.

Organization

Just as a club needs a President and a Treasurer, it needs a Legislative Chairperson—and perhaps some assistant chairpersons too.

One of the Legislative Chair's responsibilities can be to organize a telephone tree. The tree operates as a system for one person (such as the Chair) to call five people (or thereabouts) who in turn call five more people, who in turn call five more, until the whole club gets the telephone tree message—hopefully within 24 hours or less. The organizational chart for the telephone tree lists who will exactly call whom, and at what phone number. Persons who can be counted on to be especially responsible (and to call back later if the first call goes unanswered) should be placed near the beginning of the tree.

Telephone trees are used for rapid mobilization, when there's no time to wait until the next club meeting. Trees can tell members about upcoming legislative hearings, remind them to vote on election day, or urge them to attend a rally.

The importance of telephone trees is proven every legislative season, when gun club members and their friends and families pack a room to watch a hearing on a bill affecting gun rights. It makes a very powerful impression on legislators when they see the whole room filled with pro-rights citizens.

Club Meetings

Under the direction of the legislative chair, every club meeting can have a gun rights item on the agenda. The item could be the showing of a pro-rights videocassette with a group discussion afterwards; an update on national and local legislation, followed by the collection of a petition for presentation to elected officials; a letter-writing session; or the distribution of pro-rights educational material. For free supplies and ideas, contact NRA State and Local Affairs (703-267-1000), which will put you in touch with your State Liaison.

Invite Guests

Invite political candidates or officeholders to speak at your club. Candidates for races in smaller districts are most likely to say yes, and to welcome the chance to address several dozen or more voters. As always, be polite to anyone who comes to your club as a guest to speak, even if you disagree with his views.

An especially good time to invite a legislator to speak is soon after she's cast a pro-gun vote. She'll enjoy the friendly reception and applause that her vote will have earned her, and the positive reinforcement will help her stay pro-rights on the next vote.

And remember, the goodwill and friendly relations you build today with a small-town city councilwoman may pay off many times over when she is later elected to the state legislature, and perhaps later to Congress.

Elections

Once the club finds some pro-rights candidates that it likes, get behind them. Maybe the whole club can turn a Saturday afternoon meeting into a mass work session for a pro-gun candidate. Forty people working for two hours can stuff a whole lot of envelopes, drop off a lot of literature door-to-door, or put up a slew of yard signs. Seeing dozens of gun owners working en masse will make a powerful impression on any candidate, especially in local campaigns, which may only have a few volunteers active on any given day.

The weekend before and day of an election offer a good opportunity to repeat the club's mass deployment for a pro-rights candidate. The days before an election are frantic and frightening for candidates, and they will be astonished and grateful when 50 (or even 5) people show up to work at their phone bank. Of course, make sure to coordinate any club work with the candidate or the campaign manager to avoid wasted effort.

When delivering a mass of volunteers to a candidate, have them come over the club first, and then go over to campaign headquarters all together. The campaign manager will be all the more impressed by the arrival of a group of volunteers, rather than dribs and drabs.

Charity and Good Works

And of course there are plenty of good works a club can do in addition to political ones—such as organizing a toy drive for a local orphanage or children's hospital. Most club members will have some high-quality used toys at home to donate; and if each club member collects toys from a half-dozen friends at his office, church, or synagogue, you can come up with quite a haul. Alternatively, the "price" of admission for the annual Christmas party could be a toy to be donated to a child who otherwise might have nothing at Christmas.

While Christmas is the prime season for toy drives, kids love toys every day of the year. So why not make it "Christmas in July" for kids who need some help?

Everything said about the toy drive applies to food drives too. All club members can bring one or two canned food items at Thanksgiving, Christmas, or any other time of the year, and donate the food to a local organization helping the needy.

Clothes drives are useful too. Indeed, between canned food, toys, and clothes, it wouldn't be too hard to stage a drive at every club meeting. The time involved is short—just put the donated items in a box, and drive them to the recipient organization.

Club members can also volunteer to take children from orphanages or shelters to ball games, movies, bowling alleys, fireworks, and other events.

Cleanups

Police the area. No, not that kind of police. The Gun Owners ACTION Committee (from California) spent one weekend working with the Forest Service and other concerned citizens to clean up the Kentucky Shooting Area in the Angeles National Forest. The Committee provided not only workers, but also soft drinks and hot dogs for all the volunteers. By working with the Forest Service, the Committee cleaned up a badly polluted shooting area that would have been closed otherwise. Plus the Committee built up some good will on behalf of gun owners.

The Firearms Freedom Society participates in California's Adopt-a-highway litter control program. They picked up trash along a stretch of highway, and the government put up signs recognizing their efforts: "Next 1.8 miles maintained by Firearms Freedom Society."

Fundraisers

The fund-raising and charity ideas here are only the beginning. There's no limit to the ideas that you can come up with.

To raise money for the club, public affairs, or for charity, you can sell raffle tickets. The Maryland State Rifle and Pistol Association and Gun Owners of New Hampshire both have well-established raffle programs. The prizes are guns and accessories donated by pro-rights individuals or gun stores. Tickets can be sold at gun and sporting goods stores.

Auctions are another fund-raiser. The Gun Owners Action League of Massachusetts has one following its annual banquet. An annual Freedom Auction for your group might turn into a major fund-raiser if enough folks are willing to volunteer their time to make it happen. The items donated need not be gun related. A printer could donate the cost of printing business cards or invitations. An artist could do an individual's portrait. An electrician could donate four hours labor. A restaurant could donate a dinner for two.

19. The Whole Shootin' Match—and Other Public Events for Gun Clubs

"A STRONG BODY MAKES THE MIND STRONG. AS TO SPECIES OF EXERCISE, I ADVISE THE GUN. WHILE THIS GIVES MODERATE EXERCISE TO THE BODY, IT GIVES BOLDNESS, ENTERPRISE, AND INDEPENDENCE TO THE MIND. GAMES PLAYED WITH THE BALL AND OTHERS OF THAT NATURE, ARE TOO VIOLENT FOR THE BODY AND STAMP NO CHARACTER ON THE MIND. LET YOUR GUN THEREFORE BE THE CONSTANT COMPANION OF YOUR WALKS."

—Thomas Jefferson

Scheduled Competitions

The heart and soul of many gun clubs is regularly scheduled competition. In addition to the usual entrance fee, add a one or two dollar surcharge, to be sent to the NRA, or to another gun rights group.

As an alternative, give NRA members a one dollar discount on the match fee. Then ask them if you can keep the dollar and send it to the NRA Institute for Legislative Action. Most folks will readily agree.

At your matches, actively encourage participants to join the NRA, and have NRA membership materials on hand. The NRA Grassroots office (800-392-8683) can supply you with everything you need. The grassroots office can also supply the details of how the club can keep some of the revenue from new members who are signed up.

Speed Challenge

Given the (dishonest) claim by the gun prohibition lobby that semiautomatic firearms have no sporting uses, some folks have begun organizing matches designed to show the public that semiautomatics can be plenty of fun. For example, the Gun Owners ACTION Committee (862 Granite Circle, Anaheim, CA 92806) sponsors an annual "Speed Challenge and Family Shoot Day." In the speed challenge, shooters are allowed 40 rounds of ammunition, and have up to one minute to knock down 20 targets.

For people who don't want to participate in the Speed Challenge, the sponsors provide a variety of semi-automatic firearms for registrants (who pay a $10 fee) to use at the range. Lots of people who have never held an "assault weapon" in their hands before go away with an understanding that a Colt Sporter or an AKS rifle can be lots of fun.

Safety Programs

In addition to sponsoring matches among seasoned competitors, clubs need to make shooting accessible and fun for people who are new to shooting sports. If a person who has never picked up a gun before can have an enjoyable, safe experience at your range, she isn't very likely to give money to the gun prohibition lobby. In fact, she may acquire an interest in shooting, and in saving your sport.

Many clubs now have an Open Range Day, allowing community members to use the range free of charge, under supervision.

At least once a year (and preferably more often), every club should have a "Safety Day." Advertise the event to the general public, and open your club for a free day of safety instruction on safe firearms ownership. The NRA Education and Training Division can offer useful advice.

By the way, at any shooting event open to the public, don't even think of using human silhouette targets, which many people find extremely threatening. Stick only to good old-fashioned circles. Save the silhouettes for your advanced combat shooting classes.

The People's Rights Organization (Columbus, Ohio), Citizens for a Better Stockton (209-478-2525) and the Western Missouri Sportsmen's Alliance are among the numerous gun rights groups that work with local gun clubs to set up safety classes for the general public, taught by NRA-certified instructors.

Most large communities have organizations that run adult education classes: topics range from a six-hour introduction to origami folding (broken down into four classes once a week), to scuba diving, to study-tours of historic parts of town. A firearms safety class would fit in beautifully with most projects. Instructors can charge a fee that makes some money for themselves, for their club, and for the adult-education program (which pays for the catalog and advertising)—and is still reasonably priced and accessible.

NRA Day

The NRA will help you organize a public event to promote the shooting sports. For example, an Olympic shooter could put on a demonstration for the public, and talk to the audience about responsible gun ownership. For more information, contact the NRA Recruiting Program Manager at (800) 672-3888.

New Shooters Match

Many people own guns but never shoot them. If you can get them involved in shooting, you can help them realize why it is important to defend their gun rights.

One approach that some clubs take is a "New Shooters Match." The match can be IPSC-sponsored, if you so decide.

The "match" begins with classroom and instructional sessions which explain basic firearms safety rules, as well as safety rules applicable to the competition. The classroom period covers basic safety rules of the range, range commands, scoring, equipment, and basic skills.

The classroom period is followed by hands-on instruction with range officers teaching small groups. The range instructor covers topics like dealing with gun malfunctions; proper range behavior is reinforced. You'll need lots of club volunteers to serve as range officers.

The classroom plus instruction time total about three hours.

The matches are open only to individuals who have shot no more than two competitive matches. Make sure you have a supply of loaner guns available (except in jurisdictions where such loans are illegal).

For the match itself, set the targets at a close, easy-to-hit range. Award certificates to as many contestants as possible (i.e. the top 10 finishers in every category).

The NRA Recreational Shooting Division can provide you with more advice for fun events for new shooters.

Charity Match

Organize a sporting clay shoot, bowling pin shoot, or other fund-raising event for charitable purposes. Invite the media to attend the event. The event could support the local children's hospital, a battered women's shelter, or any other worthy local charity. Another good thought is raising money to send an inner-city child to summer camp in the countryside. Of course check with your intended recipient first, to make sure that they need or want your money.

Legislative/Media Shoot

Many of the reporters and television newspeople who think they hate guns have never touched one. Once they spend a little time at the firing range, their attitude about the gun issue may grow more tolerant. So invite the media out for an afternoon of shooting.

The Belmont Shooting Complex in Queensland, Australia did so, with excellent results. In conjunction with Winchester (which supplied ammunition and trophies), Belmont put on the "Winchester Inter-Media Challenge," and invited the entire local media down to the range for an afternoon of friendly competition.

Twenty-eight journalists showed up the first year, 43 the second year, and 53 the third year. Shooting events included full bore and small bore rifles, trap, and pistol contests. Targets and target ranges were modified to make beginners look good, and Belmont made sure to have a plentiful supply of ear protection, eye protection, guns, and ammunition on hand. There was also plenty of food and beer for a barbecue afterwards. The journalists loved it, and raved about it to their colleagues at work.

Media shoots can take other forms as well. If there's a semi-automatic ban proposed in your state legislature, invite the media to your gun club for a demonstration of semi-automatics. Show them the difference between a semi-automatic and an automatic, and show them how many guns look like an automatic, but don't fire like one.

If you want to know more about holding a media shoot, contact Lynne-Marie Freh at the Firearms Safety Foundation Ltd., PO Box 6111, Upper Mt. Gravatt, Queensland, 4122, Australia.

Informational shoots can take other forms as well. Invite your local legislators to a demonstration at the club to learn about guns, including the difference between a semi-automatic and an automatic. Heckler & Koch (based in Virginia) held one for Congressional staffers. The Gun Owners Action League of Massachusetts holds a shoot for state legislators and staff; the shoot also includes extensive education about firearms policy issues. Gun Owners of America puts on an annual shooting event for Washington, D.C., government employees. All of these groups would probably be delighted to offer you advice about setting up information shoots for local politicians of the media.

PART IV

STILL MORE THINGS YOU CAN DO

There are basically two kinds of people: those who put things into categories, and those who don't. As favor to the folks in the latter category, this section offers a grab-bag of different pro-rights activities that don't fit into some other general category.

20. *"The Right of the People Peaceably to Assemble"*

"WHO CAN PROTEST AN INJUSTICE BUT DOES NOT IS AN
ACCOMPLICE IN THE ACT."
                                    —The Talmud

Have you ever wanted to picket the district office of a Congressman who consistently attacks the Second Amendment, or picket the office of a television station which presents a one-sided view of the gun debate? Here's how to picket successfully.

Preparation

First, schedule a sign-making party about a day to a week before the event. The party is also a good opportunity to explain strategy and decorum. At the party, select one person who will be the group's exclusive spokesperson to the media.

It's extremely important to have one good media spokesperson. If you let anyone in the group talk to the press, then the media person editing the story will get to select which quotes from which person to use. In this case, you can be sure that, if the editor is biased, he will pick the stupidest quote from the worst-dressed person he can find.

The designated spokesperson should be able to sum up the whole issue in two sentences, and to elaborate on the topic in a less than a minute. (She still needs to know much more than one minute's worth of information, in order to deal with follow-up questions.)

At the sign-making party, have a plentiful supply of felt tip pens and large cardboard signs. Red, green, and blue are the best colors for television and newspapers. (Spurred by *USA Today*, local newspapers are using more and more color photos.)

The signs should be in good taste, and should not display prejudice of any type. If you have doubts about the propriety of a particular slogan, it's probably safer to try a different slogan.

Be sure to contact the news directors for local TV and

radio stations a few days in advance of the demonstration; call the stations again on the morning of the demonstration. Also, send out a press release to the city editors of local newspapers a few days in advance.

Publicize the picketing through the network of gun clubs, gun shows, and gun stores. The more the merrier, but a successful picketing event needs only a few people. Recognize, of course, that publicizing the picketing is going to alert the target of your plans, so don't make any contingencies based on the element of surprise.

When

Demonstrations at or before noon have the best chance of getting news coverage. Demonstrations on Monday (like anything else on Monday) are most likely to attract press attention, since there is less competition from other news.

Remember: If you've sent out press releases or otherwise informed the media earlier, give them a reminder call on the morning of the event.

Keep a close eye on other public affairs to make sure that you're not competing with an event that will draw press attention away from your demonstration. If you're picketing the city council about gun control at the same time the President is in town to give a family values award to Madonna, you may be overlooked by the media.

Sometimes a demonstration can play off the other side's event. If a gun prohibition advocate is in town, picket his speech. (But don't interfere with the speech. He has the same First Amendment rights that everyone else does.)

Where

When choosing a location, think hard about making things convenient for the press. The press is used to covering events at downtown government office buildings. They're not as likely to be willing to drive all the way to a shooting range 15 miles outside town.

The picketing site should, of course, relate to the topic you're demonstrating for. If the Mayor announced plans to deny business permits to all gun stores, picket city hall, or at a gun store.

While the First Amendment guarantees you a clear right to stage protests, the government has the authority to impose "reasonable time, place, and manner" restrictions on demonstrations on public property. Call the local police to find out about any pertinent regulations. In some public fora, such as State Capitol steps, you may have to apply for a permit several weeks in advance, and pay a fee.

Pick out a good message to chant. The chanting builds solidarity among the demonstrators, and gives the electronic media something good to cover.

Be careful not to obstruct public access to sidewalks or buildings. Likewise be careful not to obstruct access to any business.

While Picketing

While most of the demonstrators picket, one or two others should have leaflets available to hand out to interested onlookers. Otherwise, how would sympathetic passers-by know what to do next?

If passersby heckle you, don't worry about it. Don't talk to them. If you get into a confrontation with hecklers, you can be sure that the confrontation will make the news, and the main subject of the picketing will be obscured.

Maintain a good attitude at all times. It is particularly important that you be pleasant to the people who oppose you. Neutral onlookers who see picketers avoiding a confrontation with a loud-mouthed heckler will be impressed with your self-restraint and your poise—that is exactly the impression you need to convey in order to demonstrate that gun owners are responsible people.

Even if a heckler attempts to obstruct you, avoid a confrontation. Just call the police.

Finally, it's unlikely that the picketing will produce an immediate change of heart on the part of your targeted Congressperson or media outlet. The station manager is not going to run out, apologize for being so biased, and promise to start treating the Second Amendment fairly. But Congress people and the media do care intensely about public perception, and, over time, the picketing may well encourage them to have quiet thoughts about moderating their stance.

Airborne Banners

Of course picketing isn't the only way to have some fun in public. One idea that has been catching on is hiring planes to fly banners bearing a political message. The airplane can fly a message that tweaks a local politician or other official.

For instance, if you know that Senator Snerd will be giving a speech at the county fair at 2:00 p.m., you can hire a plane to fly over the fair with a message like "Snerd voted to ban 200 guns." (This message would apply to any of the 56 Senators and 216 Representatives who voted for the Feinstein/Schumer ban on so-called "assault weapons.")

Since airborne messages need to appeal to the broadest possible audience, it's even better to target some of the official's other foibles on mass-appeal issues, like taxes. For example, an airborne banner: "Snerd voted to raise taxes 27 times" should get plenty of attention, not least from Senator Snerd.

Even more than signs at demonstrations, you need to be sure that an airborne sign is factually accurate, and in good taste. If you have any questions, call your NRA State Liaison (703-267-1000) or an experienced person with another local or national gun rights group. Remember that an inaccurate or tasteless banner will redound to the benefit of the official you were attempting to criticize.

So plan carefully, and then have some good plain fun.

21. Show the Colors

> "THE DOCTRINE OF NON-RESISTANCE AGAINST ARBITRARY POWER
> AND OPPRESSION, IS ABSURD, SLAVISH, AND DESTRUCTIVE OF THE
> GOOD AND HAPPINESS OF MANKIND."
> —New Hampshire Constitution, Article 10.

One of the ways you can help build long-term support for the Second Amendment is by displaying and using pro-rights logos and messages.

Stamps

If you're older than Generation X, you may remember the "Easter Seals" and "Christmas Seals" campaigns. Charities would spend huge amounts of money to persuade folks to put a stamp with the "Easter Seals" or "Christmas Seals" logo on their mail. (The stamp had no postal value; it was purely decorative, and supplemented, but did not replace the normal U.S. Post Office stamp.)

The vast sums of money that the Easter Seals and Christmas Seals campaigns raised demonstrate the impact of these stamps. The stamps (or "seals") were especially effective because, although the stamps were printed by large organizations, the stamps were affixed by individuals. So, if you wrote a letter to your old friend Hubert and you added an "Easter Seal" to the envelope, Hubert would know that you thought highly of the Easter Seals folks. Later, when Hubert got a fundraising letter from the Easter Seals campaign (which uses the money to fight birth defects), he would already be "softened up" by the endorsement you supplied when you stuck an Easter Seal on the envelope.

Just as "Easter Seals" promoted the worthy cause of medical research, gun stamps can help promote the cause of freedom. Every time you put a gun stamp on a letter, you spread the message of freedom. (Remember, the gun stamps are purely decorative; you'll still need to add a regular postal stamp to pay for postage.) The gun stamp refutes the lie of gun prohibition lobbies who say that sentiment for repressive national gun controls is practically unanimous.

Ready to help you stamp out gun control is the Citizens Committee for the Right to Keep and Bear Arms. The stamps quote the Second Amendment to the U.S. Constitution. You can get your licks in by putting these stamps on all of your letters and correspondence. They are sold in sheets of 50 stamps, for 50 cents per sheet. To order, write CCRKBA at 12500 NE 10th Place, Bellevue, WA 98005 or call (206) 454-4911.

The National Rifle Association sells "I'm the NRA" stamps; a pack of 240 costs $4.95, plus postage and handling. You can contact the NRA Sales Department by calling (800) 336-7402, between 9 a.m. and 9 p.m., Eastern Time, Monday through Saturday, and ask for item number SS 22050. The NRA can also produce custom return address labels for you; ask the Sales Department for prices.

Checks

NRA logo checks can be ordered by calling (800) 859-1114.

More stuff

Both CCRKBA and the NRA have large merchandise catalogues, with items such as coffee mugs, jackets, ties, belt buckles, and bumper stickers. All of these items offer you an additional way to spread the pro-rights message. Ask for the NRA Member Catalogue, which you can obtain by calling (800) 336-7402.

Something as simple as wearing an NRA or CCRKBA lapel pin can be your lead-in to all sorts of pro-rights activity. For example, the November 1993 issue of the *American Rifleman* contains a letter from a respiratory therapist who started wearing his NRA lapel pin to work every day. Although a few people made critical comments, most people who saw his pin were supportive or curious. Every month, the therapist hands out a couple NRA membership applications to people who have expressed interest as a result of seeing the pin. (Instead of handing out paper applications, you could just tell people to call 1-800-336-7402; or call the number yourself, and ask for a packet of membership applications.) The pin also provided a starting point for folks who wanted to ask about where to attend firearms safety training; and for a school board member who wanted to learn more about the NRA's Eddie Eagle Gun Safety program.

Of course you don't need to order merchandise to display the pro-rights message. Some folks personalize their license plates, with messages such "JOIN NRA" or "2ND AMEND."

Many office-supply stores will make a rubber stamp for you with a custom message of your choice. The stamp can then be used to beautify envelopes and other surfaces with pro-rights slogans, such as "Gun control is people control" or "I'm the NRA" or "Support the Second Amendment" or any other short slogan you like.

Likewise, party supply stores will often manufacture custom buttons for you, displaying the slogan of your choice. Order a few dozen, and give them away to your pro-rights friends.

A little imagination can go a long way. One gun-owner, who also happens to be a model railroad hobbyist, painted one of his model train cars with the words "Second Amendment." When he displays the car at railroad shows, folks come by to ask him questions about gun rights and gun control.

Readers who use computer electronic mail know that it's pretty easy to custom design your own e-mail logo, which will accompany every e-mail message you send. Why not make a pro-rights message into your logo?

Another good thing to hand out to folks who are interested in the gun issue is the NRA Firearms Fact Card. This little tri-fold card, which easily fits inside a wallet, contains plenty of basic information about the gun issue. It supplies an excellent starting point of information for folks who are curious about the real facts. You can order the Fact Card in bulk by calling the NRA Sales Department at 1-800-336-7402, and asking for item NL 00890; they'll send you up to 25 for free.

The NRA also has lots of other free brochures that are

useful for educating yourself and others. They include: "How Media Misinformation Threatens Your Rights" (item IL 00680); "Semi-Auto Firearms: The Citizen's Choice" (IL 00540); and "Ten Myths About Gun Control" (IL 00920).

Betsy Ross

Some pro-rights folks have taken to flying the "Betsy Ross Flag," the thirteen star flag that was the first flag of the United States. They fly the flag as a protest against the encroachments of current governments on rights guaranteed by our Constitution and as a reminder of the American values of independence and freedom that created our country. Among the many flag stores that sells Betsy Ross Flags is The Flag Center, 2267 Massachusetts Ave., Cambridge, MA 02140. (800) 367 3710. The flag costs $30.90 from these folks.

Merv Griffin

Finally, remember the advice that Merv Griffin's mother always gave him: "Merv, don't be a jerk." If you're displaying a pro-rights bumper sticker, lapel pin, or other paraphernalia, be nice. If you put an NRA bumper sticker on your car, and then go around cutting off other cars, riding their tail, and acting like a New Jersey driver when you're in Oklahoma City, you're a walking advertisement for anti-gun lobby. Displaying pro-gun materials, like gun ownership itself, requires that you show yourself to be a responsible, considerate person, a walking advertisement for the mature, thoughtful behavior of gun owners.

22. *Make it Your Business to Care*

"FOR THE SADDEST EPITAPH WHICH CAN BE CARVED IN MEMORY
OF A VANISHED FREEDOM IS THAT IT WAS LOST BECAUSE ITS POS-
SESSORS FAILED TO STRETCH FORTH A SAVING HAND WHILE THERE
WAS STILL TIME."
—Supreme Court Justice George Sutherland.

Think about what you can do to get your business or your
professional skills involved.

Perhaps there's a fundraising project you could do. Does
your business have telephones that could be used as phone bank
for get-out-and-vote calling at election time? Maybe you're a
printer who can donate free or low-cost printing services to a
local gun group. Or are you an artist who can help a group with
its graphic design projects? Could your company's computers be
used by a gun rights group to maintain a database of members or
voters?

Maybe your company can set up a matching gift program
for employees who want to donate to pro-rights organizations.
Alternatively, the company could pay 50% of an employee's annual dues for NRA, the Second Amendment Foundation, the Citizens Committee for the Right to Keep and Bear Arms, or another
pro-rights group.

Could a company meeting room be made available to a
local gun group to make a presentation to interested employees?

Some businesses offer discounts to members of NRA or
other pro-gun groups. For example, Michael de Bethencourt's
defense training company, in North Billerica, Mass., lets anyone
who joins the Gun Owners Action League of Massachusetts de-
duct the one-year membership fee from the cost of tuition.

You don't need to run a gun-related business to offer a
discount. Your accounting, catering, or insurance company could
give a discount to gun group members, or pledge to donate a
percentage of revenues from gun group members to pro-gun organizations.

A restaurant owner could offer to donate 5% of the cost of each meal to a local rights group (or to NRA/ILA, CCRKBA, or any other gun group that you like) for every NRA membership card holder that comes in.

Happily, you can do well by doing good; local grassroots gun groups will probably be delighted to give you discount advertising in their newsletter, informing the members about your pro-rights activity.

Employees

One of the most painless ways for people to give money to good causes is by giving a little at a time—such as an automatic paycheck deduction. Over the course of the year, they end up making a good-sized gift (and earning a good-sized tax deduction). So consider offering your employees a mechanism for making charitable contributions by payroll deduction.

If you want help setting such a program up, ask your local United Way for help; they raise millions of dollars each year through workplace campaigns. In fact, you could ask the United Way to set up a program to allow employees to designate money to one (or more) of the tax-exempt organizations listed in chapter 5.

If you do set up a workplace program, remember that participation should be strictly voluntary. Ideally, the only persons who should have access to information about who is giving how much to which charity should be the people who need to know (like the payroll department). After all, since the pro-rights movement is based on individual freedom and personal choice, it would be wrong to raise money for that movement by infringing on other people's freedom.

Attorneys

The Second Amendment Foundation maintains a list of lawyers who have an interest in taking cases that relate to guns and gun rights. Every month, SAF receives a large number of calls from its members and the public seeking legal advice and services. If you are a lawyer, the Attorney Referral Service puts your name in front of potential clients. Over 400 attorneys across the nation have signed up for this program, which costs them nothing. If you are interested in having your name on the list, contact the Attorney Referral Service, SAF, 12500 NE 10th Place, Bellevue, WA 98005 or call (206) 454-7012.

The NRA also maintains a referral program, which helps people not only with firearm law cases, but also with land-use laws and shooting range problems. You can receive an information packet by sending a short note, written on your letterhead, to: NRA Attorney Referral Program, Office of the NRA General Counsel, 11250 Waples Mill Road, Fairfax, VA., 22030.

If you are an attorney with expertise in estate planning and taxes, you can make your services available *pro bono* to persons who wish to participate in the NRA's planned giving program. Contact: Planning and Development, NRA, 12500 Waples Mill Road, Fairfax, VA, 22030. (703) 267-1000.

The Lyndhurst, New Jersey law firm of DeClemente, Topolski & Terlizzi offers 20% discounts on legal services to the members of the NRA or of the Association of New Jersey Rifle and Pistol Clubs. Perhaps your firm could attract some new clients by publicizing a similar discount in your local gun-rights organization's newsletter.

23. Other Pro-Freedom Groups

"WHO WILL STAND GUARD TO THE GUARDS THEMSELVES?"—
Juvenal.

While we've already urged you to support the national pro-gun groups (in our first book), we'd be remiss if we didn't urge you to support other pro-freedom groups.

The right to bear arms is the issue which animates this book, but it would be foolish to view the right to bear arms in isolation. While some anti-gunners imagine that the Second Amendment can be destroyed while other freedoms remain intact, in reality an attack upon one Amendment is an attack upon all. The Bill of Rights is a magnificent tapestry of freedom, and when one thread unravels, the whole tapestry deteriorates.

Accordingly, persons who support the Second Amendment ought to be enthusiastic advocates of the rest of the Constitution, including the provisions on property rights, freedom of religion, free speech, and freedom from unreasonable search and seizure.

When "conservatives" assault the right to habeas corpus and the right of criminal suspects to remain silent, they endanger the Constitution just as much as "liberals" who attack property rights and state rights. As former Colorado Attorney General Duane Woodard observed, there is no liberal Constitution and no conservative Constitution. There is just one Constitution, and every portion of it deserves our full support.

Take every opportunity you can get to network with other organizations. The anti-gun organizations do an excellent job of this. In our case, the organizations to reach out to are those that support limited government. For example, a local grassroots organization working to limit taxes may have many members sympathetic to gun rights.

Families Against Mandatory Minimums

Instead of banning guns, why not enact laws imposing

severe mandatory sentences on all criminals? A great idea, say many gun owners, but one that is tragically wrong.

Even when applied to people who committed crimes in the past, mandatory minimums can cause a miscarriage of justice.

For example, the federal Armed Career Criminal Act imposes severe mandatory minimum prison terms on ex-felons who possess firearms. The law is triggered by the mere possession of a firearm, not by the use of a gun in a crime.

In one recent Indiana case, a man named David Eubank, who had served a prison sentence for robbery, was released and put on probation. He went straight, and checked in regularly with his probation officer. Later, Eubank asked the officer if it was all right to get a .22 rifle to hunt for food, the probation officer said yes.

The probation officer was correct under Indiana law, which allows ex-felons to own long guns, but was incorrect under federal law, which bars all gun possession by ex-felons.

A while later, Indiana police and federal officials raided Eubank's home, searching for evidence that he was committing robberies again. They found not one iota of such evidence, but they did find a .22 rifle. So the federal government prosecuted him, threatening a longer term for possessing the gun (after his probation officer told him it was all right) than he would have served if he actually perpetrated more robberies! After surviving several months in jail while awaiting trial, Eubank went to court and was acquitted.

In an El Paso case, Bill Keagle, who committed burglaries in 1978, went straight after release from prison. Unaware of the federal Act, Keagle took a .22 rifle and a shotgun he owned down to a pawnshop and sold them. As part of the sale, he filled out the federal gun registration document, Form 4473. Since Keagle sold the guns, and was willing to fill out a registration form when he did so, he obviously had no criminal intent.

However, this didn't stop the El Paso police and the federal government from finding the 4473 form and throwing the book at him. In exchange for dropping charges, which would have led to a 15 year mandatory minimum, Keagle was forced to accept an eight year prison sentence.

In Massachusetts, everyone who possesses a gun or ammunition needs a license, but the license is relatively easy to obtain. Accordingly, the state government, figuring that anyone who wouldn't voluntarily pass through the licensing process must be a bad actor, created a mandatory one-year minimum sentence for the violation of gun control laws.

The son of New Hampshire State Representative David Welch (R-Kingston) lived in New Hampshire, but worked in Massachusetts. While he was driving home from work one day, he was stopped for a traffic offense, and the police found five shotgun shells in his car (no gun, just the shells). The young man was threatened with a mandatory one-year prison term for violation of the gun control laws. Happily, young Welch's lawyer found a way for his client to evade the mandatory minimum.

As Larry Pratt, head of Gun Owners of America, points out, passage of fully informed jury laws would mitigate much of the harshness of mandatory minimums. If jurors were informed that convicting the defendant would subject him to a draconian prison sentence, and that it is their legal right to vote their conscience and acquit under any circumstances, then jurors would spare many fellow citizens from the worst applications of mandatory minimums.

But aren't mandatory minimums necessary because most judges are too soft on criminals? Not these days. It is true that in the past, some judges, such as Washington, D.C.'s David Bazelon, thought that most criminals shouldn't be punished, because they had deprived childhoods.

Today, such judges have almost entirely disappeared. The vast majority of modern federal judges have been appointed by Presidents Bush or Reagan, and take an extremely hard line in favor of prosecutors. Saying that we need mandatory minimums today to overcome liberal judges is like saying we need to increase the defense budget to guard against Mussolini.

Perhaps mandatory minimums don't seem like much of a

problem for folks who don't have a felony record, or who stay away from places like Massachusetts. But the fact is, mandatory minimums threaten the safety of every single American.

While your taxes increased in the last decade to pay for the doubling of the national prison capacity, a huge amount of the prison space went to incarcerate people for non-violent offenses like gun possession. Today, prisons are bursting at the seams and there is little room for hard-core, violent criminals because the space is already taken by non-violent criminals serving mandatory minimums.

Mandatory minimums are the best thing that ever happened to violent criminals, because mandatory minimums prevent today's judges from doing what they want—putting violent thugs away for a long time—and force the prison system to waste precious space on non-violent offenders. Next time someone you know is mugged by a violent criminal out on parole, thank the legislators who created your state's mandatory minimums for gun possession and other non-violent offenses, and thereby forced the early release of the violent criminal.

If you agree that mandatory minimums benefit nobody except violent criminals, then consider joining a new organization, Families Against Mandatory Minimums (FAMM). Send a donation of any size you would like to FAMM at 1001 Pennsylvania Ave NW, Suite 200 South, Washington DC 20004. (202) 457-5790. (If you make the check out to the "FAMM Foundation," it's tax-deductible.

FAMM has grown rapidly, and is at the forefront of the drive to fix America's irrational sentencing laws. FAMM's director, Julie Stewart, who formerly worked with the Cato Institute, is 100% opposed to gun control, and is a strong supporter of the Second Amendment.

If you'd like to learn more about mandatory minimums, pick up a copy of Dave Kopel's, "Prison Blues: How America's Foolish Sentencing Policies Endanger Public Safety." You can get it for four dollars from the Cato Institute, 1000 Mass. Ave NW, Washington, DC 20001. (202) 842-0200.

And while you're at it, sign-up for a $50 membership with Cato, the best pro-liberty think tank in the known universe.

Part V

Teach Your Children (and everyone else) Well

Protecting the right to bear arms means more than just writing letters to Congress. It also means nurturing and enhancing the culture of responsible gun ownership in the United States. Being a good gun rights defender also means being a responsible gun owner, and helping to teach responsibility to everyone, particularly to younger generations. Responsibility also means helping younger generations learn the truth about the right to keep and bear arms in American history and in modern America.

24. Essay Contests

"IF YOU ARE THINKING A YEAR AHEAD, SOW SEED. IF YOU ARE THINKING TEN YEARS AHEAD, PLANT A TREE. IF YOU ARE THINKING ONE HUNDRED YEARS AHEAD, EDUCATE THE PEOPLE."—Chinese proverb.

Work with your local school, or some other child-oriented organization (such as the local Boy Scouts or Girl Scouts) to set up a Second Amendment Essay contest.

For all the children who enter the contest, writing the essay will help them focus their thoughts on the right to bear arms and gun control, and encourage them to consider the issue more logically. Remember, the more logic that is applied to the issue, the better for our side.

Five hundred words is a good word limit, and can be adjusted down for lower grades, up for higher ones.

Good topic questions should be open-ended, and not force ideological essays. For example, "Why is the Second Amendment Important to our Nation?" will generate lots of essays about gun ownership for protection. But if a student wants to write an essay about why the National Guard is a "well-regulated militia," and why the National Guard is important, he still can.

If the National Guard aficionado writes the best essay, then award him the prize. Prizes should be based on good writing and argumentation, not ideological correctness.

There are two groups which have experience with essay contests and can give you some advice. The People's Rights Organization of Columbus, Ohio, sponsors a Second Amendment Essay Contest in the Columbus schools, and offers $2,000 in prizes for the winners.

The PRO-Second Amendment group in Grand Junction, Colorado runs a similar contest for the schools in its county. The winners receive cash prizes, donated by local archery and gun stores, at the group's annual banquet. PRO gives the winner an extra morale boost by printing the winning essays in its newsletter.

The Second Amendment Foundation (206-454-7012) will send you commemorative coins to distribute to contest participants.

If you can't get a contest running at your local school, perhaps you can make students and teachers aware of a national contest they could enter: The NRA's Firearms and Civil Rights Legal Defense Fund sponsors annual essay contests for elementary, junior high, and senior high school students. Top prize in each category is a thousand dollar savings bond. Essays for the year's topic are generally due at the end of each May. For more information, contact FCRLDF Essay Desk, 11250 Waples Mill Road, Fairfax, VA 22030. The Essay Desk can supply a list of reference aids to assist students participating in the contest.

The FCRLDF also sponsors a writing contest for law students. First prize is a year's tuition at law school! For more information, contact the FCRLDF at the address above, or call (703) 267-1250.

25. *Textbook Accuracy*

"TO KNOW NOTHING OF WHAT HAPPENED BEFORE YOU WERE BORN
IS TO REMAIN EVER A CHILD."

—Cicero

As political correctness takes over American education, history textbooks are increasingly being written by people who push their own leftist ideological predilections at the expense of an accurate portrayal of our nation's past.

Many history textbooks now spout the ridiculous line that the Second Amendment was written so that the *government* (the National Guard) could have guns. As this fraud is spread to school-children, your rights become weaker and weaker in the long run. You can be sure that a textbook which makes basic errors about one part of our nation's struggle for freedom has plenty of other errors.

For example, the textbook by J.W. Peltason, *Understanding the Constitution* (published by Holt, Rinehart, and Winston, Inc.), spends 33 pages on the First Amendment, but less than a single page on the Second Amendment. The page contains the plainly false statement that the Second Amendment was *not* "designed to prevent [the federal government] from regulating private ownership of arms."

Handgun Control, Inc. is working hard to get nonsense like this into school textbooks, and to make sure that anti-gun textbooks are the ones used in every school in the country.

Get involved in your local school's textbook selection process. Almost every government school has some kind of textbook selection committee open to members of the public. If your children attend private or religious schools, there may also be a way for you to get involved, formally or informally, in textbook review. The NRA-ILA Research office and the Second Amendment Foundation can supply you with reprints of plenty of scholarly articles detailing the historical origins of the Second Amendment.

They'll also be happy to give you advice if you run into a conflict in your work for accurate history textbooks. You can contact Project Textbooks, NRA-ILA, 11250 Waples Mill Road, Fairfax, VA 22030. When you write to Project Textbooks, make sure to note the textbook's title, edition, author, and publisher and make photocopies of the relevant pages of the textbook.

26. Be a Good Teacher

"To preserve liberty it is essential that the whole body of the people always possess arms and be taught alike, especially when young, how to use them."

—Richard Henry Lee.

The quote at the top of this page really says it all. One very important way to defend the right to keep and bear arms is to help expand the number of people who know how to exercise that right.

Friends and Neighbors

Next time you plan to go to the range, or a bowling pin shoot, or a skeet tournament, ask one of your friends or neighbors to come along. For so many people, the only time they ever see a gun is on television—where the images are almost entirely negative. Network television and many newspapers completely ignore all shooting sports (except for a little attention paid to hunting). When you bring a non-shooting friend to a target match, he'll see that shooting is family activity, and that gun-owners—rather than strutting around in Nazi regalia—look just like everybody else. One trip to the range won't convince your friend to become a life member of the NRA, but the trip will help him see the wholesome side of guns.

NRA Instructor

If you know a lot about shooting, and enjoy working with people, become an NRA Certified Instructor. You can teach classes (or give personal instruction) in Rifle, Pistol, Shotgun, Home Firearm Safety, Muzzleloading Rifle, Muzzleloading Pistol, Muzzleloading Shotgun, or Personal Protection. To find out more, contact the NRA, Training Department, at (703) 267-3808.

If you already are an NRA Certified Instructor, Coach, or Training Counselor, you're in a great position to recruit new NRA members. And you earn ten dollars for every new member and five dollars for every renewal you send in. To find out more, call (703) 267-3784.

Children

Teaching younger people how to shoot can seem daunting, especially if you haven't been around shooting-age children for a while. But while adolescents (like guns) can seem terrifying to people who are unfamiliar them, they can be quite a lot of fun, if treated properly.

Fortunately, there are lots of folks with plenty of experience at running youth programs. The NRA Safety and Education Division has a brochure called "How to Organize a Youth Shooting Program." It's available for two dollars by calling 1-800-336-7402. You can also obtain a comprehensive "NRA Rifle Shooting Sports Safety Kit," designed to facilitate youth programs with smallbore rifles, air rifles, and BB guns. The kit sells for $40.

Plenty of independent (non-Boy Scout) summer camp shooting programs need youth shooting instructors. If you can help, the NRA has a "job bank" for camps that could use your services. Contact the NRA's Safety and Education Division (703-267-1000). The Safety and Education Division also runs an NRA Coach Program, which teaches you how to be a high-quality shooting coach. Contact the Coach Program Specialist at the Safety and Education Division.

If you'd like to set up a shooting program for Girl Scouts, contact Cathy Tolley, 862 Granite Circle, Anaheim, CA 92806, who set up an instruction and skills program for Girl Scouts in her area.

Junior NRA

If you don't have the time to take an aspiring young shooter down to the range, you can still buy them a Junior Membership to the National Rifle Association. The membership costs 15 dollars, per year, and entitles the member to a subscription to the junior shooting magazine *Insights*. When donating the membership, you can pay an additional $15, entitling the junior member to also receive *American Rifleman* or *American Hunter.* Spend the extra money for the *Rifleman/Hunter* subscription; these magazines have important information about gun rights that does not appear in *Insights*, which attempts to stay scrupulously apolitical. You can buy someone a membership by calling toll-free (800) 672-3888.

Jaycees Educational Programs

The Jaycees (the United States Junior Chamber of Commerce) and Daisy Manufacturing Company (Rogers, Ark.) co-sponsor an outstanding shooting education program. Jaycees from the ages of 8 to 15 can participate in a gun safety program (covering education, safety, enjoyment, and competition), which then allows them to participate in BB gun target-shooting teams. The teams compete for state championships, and the top three teams in each state then compete at the International BB Gun Championship Match in July. More than 12 million boys and girls have successfully completed the Shooting Education program

To find out more about setting up or helping with this fine program, contact the U.S. Junior Chamber of Commerce Shooting Education department at (918) 584-2481. Or you can write to the Shooting Education department, at PO Box 7, Tulsa, OK 74121-0007.

Eddie Eagle

You would never know it from reading the newspapers, but the fatal firearm accident rate for children ages 0-14 has fallen from 550 in 1975 to 220 in 1992. (Source: the National Safety Council's book *Accident Facts*). You can further this copacetic trend by promoting the Eddie Eagle firearms safety program. While the NRA has always had junior shooting and hunting programs that emphasize the development of safe sporting gun use under adult supervision, the organization launched a safety campaign in 1988 that was aimed at the millions of children who never have any exposure to shooting sports. The creator of the program, NRA First vice-president Marion Hammer, won a public service award from the National Safety Council—proof of the program's excellent quality.

The Eddie Eagle program is geared towards children in pre-school through 6th grade. Using teacher-tested materials such as an animated video, cartoon workbooks, role-playing, and fun safety activities, Eddie Eagle teaches the simple lesson: "If you see a gun, stop! Don't touch it. Leave the area. Tell an adult." Or, in the three word summary: "No, Go, Tell."

Over four million children and parents have participated in Eddie Eagle through schools, law-enforcement programs, and other youth programs. Unfortunately, Eddie Eagle has been excluded from some schools by politically-correct administrators whose hatred of the NRA's support for the Second Amendment outweighs their concern with child safety. Notably, Eddie Eagle contains no political content.

One good thing you can do for the next generation is work to get the program adopted in your local school.

If the bureaucracy at your school is too hysterical about guns to allow a pro-safety educational program to take place on school property, set up your own program. Work with some local, friendly teachers to set up an Eddie Eagle event one afternoon after school. Invite the Boy Scouts, Girl Scouts, or any other group of kids. You can get free sample materials, and other assistance, for setting up an Eddie Eagle program by calling (800) 231-0752. To order Eddie Eagle materials, call (800) 336-7402.

The Georgia State Legislature, by the way, has passed a resolution encouraging all elementary schools in the state to participate in the Eddie Eagle program. Perhaps you might want to encourage your local city council or other government body to do the same.

While Eddie Eagle has nothing to do with politics, and everything to do with safety, just the opposite is true about some other so-called "gun safety" programs. For example, the Milwaukee police, in conjunction with McDonald's, have produced a ridiculous cartoon "safety" book featuring talking, animated guns with names like "Sammy Saturday Night Special." The use of talking guns (in contrast to Eddie Eagle's realistic, inanimate guns) obviously detracts from the realism and the effectiveness of the gun safety message.

Moreover, the comic book tells children to call the police if they find a gun in their parent's home. In the Milwaukee/McDonald's comic, the gun that triggers the phone call happens to be a stolen one, which the father bought without knowing it was "hot." But the children didn't know that, nor did the police in the comic, until they had seized the gun, and taken it in for tracing.

So there's your choice in gun safety: the Eddie Eagle program which teaches your children to be safe, or Milwaukee-style programs which teaches your children to be government informants.

Teaching History

Finally, if you're one of the increasing numbers of participants in historical re-enactments and old-time shooting shows, perhaps you can talk to a schoolroom about subjects such as "What Was Life Like for a Mountain Man?" or "What Was It Like to Fight in Civil War?" The kids will get a kick out of your authentic regalia. And if the school consents, you can bring along an (unloaded) black powder or other period firearm. (Make sure to comply with the federal and state "gun-free school zone" laws, some of which are so stupid as to prohibit your bringing an unloaded blackpowder rifle to school for instructional purposes.) The students won't learn anything about modern gun control issues, but they will see one aspect of the honorable role guns have played in America's heritage.

To get yourself more engagements for your firearms and history presentation, sign up with the NRA Gun Collector's Speakers Bureau. (It's a subdivision of the NRA's Education and Training Division.) Conversely, if you want to bring a firearms and history speaker to your school, the Speaker's Bureau is a great referral source.

Remember, if you don't teach the next generation the good side of guns, the hatemongers from the gun control lobbies will be teaching them to fear guns and hate gun owners.

27. *On Campus*

"IF IT BE ADMITTED THAT A MAN, POSSESSING ABSOLUTE POWER, MAY MISUSE THAT POWER BY WRONGING HIS ADVERSARIES, WHY SHOULD A MAJORITY NOT BE LIABLE TO THE SAME REPROACH? MEN ARE NOT APT TO CHANGE THEIR CHARACTERS BY AGGLOMERATION; NOR DOES THEIR PATIENCE IN THE PRESENCE OF OBSTACLES INCREASE WITH THE CONSCIOUSNESS OF THEIR STRENGTH. AND FOR THESE REASONS I CAN NEVER WILLINGLY INVEST ANY NUMBER OF MY FELLOW CREATURES WITH THAT UNLIMITED AUTHORITY WHICH I SHOULD REFUSE TO ANY ONE OF THEM."— Alexis do Tocqueville.

Our previous book detailed how to form a gun rights group. All of the suggestions from that chapter apply to campus groups as well. Here are some other suggestions geared especially towards campus groups.

First of all, look at the existing groups on your campus, particularly the ones involved in public affairs. Watch what they do, and see how it works. Imitation is the sincerest form of flattery.

Putting up leaflets around campus and placing an ad in the campus newspaper are good ways to alert people about a new group, and to invite them to attend the first meeting.

Scheduling meeting times and places will be relatively easy, since all students are on campus already. As social relationships offer important incentives for people to get and stay involved, consider scheduling some meetings during meals: "The Gorgonzola University Second Amendment Society will meet at 6 p.m., in dining room C of the main cafeteria."

Check out your student government's regulations involving campus organizations. Once you get certified as an official campus organization, you can often get financial support for your activities.

In setting the tone for your organization, try to be consistent with other types of groups already on campus. For example, if your college campus already has advocacy groups like Democratic Socialists of America, Young Republicans, and the like, then the student government could not have a legitimate objection to your new "Gun Rights Protection Alliance."

In contrast, if your high school doesn't have political groups, and instead has only groups like the Physics Club, the Business Club, and the Debate Society, then structure your organization along a more neutral, academic line, such as the "Second Amendment Research Society." Of course, to keep your group in good standing, adhere to the guidelines you set forth in order to get the club certified.

Particularly in high school, many people are involved in extra-curricular activities not only for the activities' own merit, but also to boost their resume (for college applications). Accept this fact; use it to your advantage by delegating responsibility to as many people as you can.

Other Activities

Of course, there are plenty of other ways you can raise consciousness about the Second Amendment on campus. You can:

Create an independent study project with a faculty member.

Ask a teacher to make the right to bear arms part of the curriculum.

Urge other groups on campus to pass a resolution urging your elected officials to support the entire Bill of Rights, including the right to bear arms. Send the officials a copy of the resolution when it passes.

Organize a student-run right to bear arms course.

Sponsor a speech or debate involving the right to bear arms. A friendly teacher may offer extra credit for attending the program, and might even integrate the program into the week's lesson plan.

Ask your history, civics, or political science teacher to devote a period to the Second Amendment. The format could be a debate, a discussion, an essay, or writing letters to elected officials.

If your school participates in a Model Government or similar program, wherein students pretend to be legislators or convention delegates, propose a pro-Second Amendment resolution to be adopted.

Write an article for your school newspaper.

See what books your library has on the Second Amendment. If they only have a few, suggest that your librarian buy some of the books discussed in chapter 13 and in *Things You Can Do the Defend Your Gun Rights*. A good choice for a library that can only afford one book and wants to get both points of view is, *The Gun Control Debate: You Decide*, by Lee Nisbet (Amherst, NY: Prometheus Books).

When you choose a subject for a school report or essay, write about gun rights, or some other angle of gun ownership. The books listed in chapter 13 and in our previous book provide a good resource for research on your paper.

Even if you're not old enough to vote, write to your elected officials (The previous book has writing tips). Letters from youth, because they're so rare, often attract more attention from politicians than do letters from older folks.

28. *Your Own Project*

"WHEN THE GOVERNMENT FEARS THE PEOPLE, THERE IS LIB-
ERTY. WHEN THE PEOPLE FEAR THE GOVERNMENT, THERE IS TYR-
ANNY."—Thomas Jefferson

When Peruvian dictator Alberto Fujimori came to San
Francisco in 1991, Amnesty International was on hand; the group
hired a small plane to circle overhead, trailing a banner "Pres.
Fujimori: Restore Human Rights to Peru."

There is no limit to the creative projects you can under-
take. Don't hesitate to call the NRA Grassroots Office or the Citizens Committee for the Right to Keep and Bear Arms, if you
want to run your idea by an experienced activist.

While remaining faithful to your conviction, be flexible in
your strategies.

Whatever your project, keep in mind the principles discussed throughout this book: careful preparation, good manners,
and seeing things from the other person's point of view.

Part VI

Civic Duties and Morality

We started writing this book in the summer of 1990, and we're finishing it early in 1995. Lots of things have happened in those five years, but the fundamentals remain the same. Until the end of history, the details will change, but the basic principles underlying the struggle for freedom will not.

This concluding section is the longest part of the book because it is the most important. Having improved your skills as a gun rights activist, what are the great truths that should animate you actions?

The principle of responsible citizenship underlies everything. Play a responsible part in the criminal justice system. Be alert not just to immediate dangers, but also to long-term threats to freedom. A responsible citizen is a hard-working, vigorous freedom-fighter—a freedom-fighter who understands the essential moral difference between wanting to defeat the opposition and hating it. One person at a time, we can build an ever-widening circle of tolerance, charity, and hope.

29. Be a Fully Informed Juror

"I CONSIDER TRIAL BY JURY AS THE ONLY ANCHOR YET IMAGINED BY MAN BY WHICH A GOVERNMENT CAN BE HELD TO THE PRINCIPLES OF ITS CONSTITUTION."—Thomas Jefferson.

"In this country, we have three ways to secure our freedom," remarked former Idaho Senator Steve Symms, "The ballot box, the jury box, and if those don't work, the cartridge box." This chapter discusses how doing your legal duties in the jury box can help protect your right to own a cartridge box.

A few years ago, in Oak Park, Illinois, a gas station owner drew a gun to defend himself against an armed robbery. Oak Park has a handgun ban, so the prosecutor threw the book at the gas station owner. A jury speedily acquitted him, although the facts seemed to clearly prove the station owner guilty.

Was the jury acting illegally? Not at all. The jury was simply exercising its power to judge the law as well as the facts. The jury apparently determined that in the particular case, it would be unjust to punish the gas station owner for violating the handgun prohibition.

In one infamous prosecution under the Gun Control Act of 1968, the federal government brought 88 felony charges against a skeet shooter who sold guns as hobby to pay for some of his shooting expenses. The "crimes" worth 88 felony counts and up to 440 years in prison? Letting his customers practice with the guns for a few days before buying them, and making gun sales at the range rather than at his business office. Although the defendant admitted his actions on the stand—his acts were technical violations of the Gun Control Act—the jury found him "not guilty" on every count.

Jury acquittal of a defendant who is technically guilty, but who does not deserve punishment, is called "jury nullification." In the American legal system, the jury's power to nullify is unquestionable.

The District of Columbia Court of Appeals—the second highest court in the United States—explains that the jury has an "unreviewable and irreversible power...to acquit in disregard of the instruction on the law given by the trial judge..." (*U.S.* v. *Dougherty*, 473 F.2d 1139 (1972).) Or as another federal court of appeals summarizes: "If the jury feels the law under which the defendant is accused is unjust, or that exigent circumstances justified the action of the accused, or for any reason which appeals to their logic or passion, the jury has the power to acquit and the courts must abide by that decision." (*United States* v. *Moylan*, 417 F.2d 1002, 1006 (4th Cir. 1969).)

The court was re-affirming what John Jay, the first Chief Justice of the U.S. Supreme Court, told jurors: they possess "a right...to determine the law as well as the fact in controversy." (*Georgia* v. *Brailsford* 3 Dallas 1, 4 (1794).)

The most common situations for nullification are self-defense and defense of property, when prosecutors throw the book at crime victims who might have technically exceeded legal boundaries.

The Rule of Law

Columbia Law Professor George Fletcher observes that jury nullification might at first seem "to conflict with the rule of law, but careful historical reflection underscores the power of the jury not to defeat the law, but to perfect the law, to realize the law's inherent values." He points to the jury acquittal of John Peter Zenger in a 1735 trial for seditious libel. ("Seditious libel" was the criminal offense of harming a government official's reputation.) Zenger's lawyer told the jury that they were the ultimate judges of law as well as fact; the jury acquitted Zenger on the grounds that his articles in *The New York Weekly Journal* about a corrupt governor were true—even though the formal law did not yet recognize truth as a defense to seditious libel. (George Fletcher, *A Crime of Self-Defense: Bernhard Goetz and the Law on Trial* (New York: Free Press, 1988).)

That's how the American system works; the law is created by "We the People." If a power-hungry prosecutor exercises bad judgment, the people, acting through the jury, can stop him.

Jurors' Duty

Accordingly, it is not only the juror's right, but her obligation to vote her conscience. As John Adams explained before he was elected president, it is the juror's "duty...to find the verdict according to his own best understanding judgment, and conscience, though in direct opposition to the direction of the court."

Two state Constitutions explicitly affirm jury rights. Maryland's Constitution recognizes the jury as "the Judges of Law, as well as of fact." (Maryland Const., Declaration of Rights, Art. 23.) Indiana's Constitution states that "the jury shall have the right to determine the law and the facts." (Indiana Const., Art. I, § 19.)

Curiously, although there is no legal doubt about the jury's right to vote its conscience and acquit, there is generally no rule that the jury be told about that right. In 1895, a divided Supreme Court held that there was no Constitutional requirement that juries be informed of their power to nullify. (*Spars and Hanson*, 156 U.S. 64.) The case came from an era when the Court was devoted to protecting corporate power. Going on strike or joining a union was generally illegal, but juries were refusing to convict workers accused of these "crimes."

Checks and Balances

The jury's right and duty to vote its conscience is one of the most important checks in our system of checks and balances. Accordingly, the Fully Informed Jury Amendment has drawn support from an amazingly diverse coalition of groups. Tree-hugging EarthFirsters attend FIJA meetings with timber-cutting Wise Use advocates. Radical pro-abortion feminists sit next to Eagle Forum anti-feminists.

Interestingly, while anti-nuclear and pacifist groups are also part of the FIJA coalition, the anti-gun movement is not. Perhaps the anti-gun lobby fears that fully informed juries would be a significant obstacle to enforcement of repressive gun control laws.

Accordingly, the Fully Informed Jury Amendment is supported by many pro-Second Amendment groups, including the National Rifle Association, Gun Owners of America, Neal Knox's Firearms Coalition, the Gun Owners Action League of Massachusetts, and the American Pistol and Rifle Association. FIJA was also endorsed at the 1990 Gun Rights Policy Conference sponsored by the Second Amendment Foundation and the Citizens Committee for the Right to Keep and Bear Arms.

These groups recognize that the whole Bill of Rights is one magnificent and interwoven tapestry of freedom. When we protect the rights of juries, we protect the rights of all other citizens as well, including gun owners.

To find out more, contact the Fully Informed Jury Association: Their 24 hour national hotline is (314) 997-8588. FIJA National Headquarters is at PO Box 59, Helmville, Montana 59843. (406) 793-5550. The national headquarters can steer you to one of the many state-wide groups active in the issue.

When They Come for You

By the way, what if you're ever on the receiving end of the criminal justice system? Perhaps you were driving from your home in Pennsylvania to go hunting in Maine. As you passed through New York City, you saw a rape in progress, and took out your gun to frighten away the rapist. The police, arriving long after the rapist escaped, are now wondering whether to arrest you for possession of an unregistered weapon. Cases like this happen all the time, and not just in New York City.

In such a situation (or in another situation in which, as a free American citizen, you simply don't want be hassled by the police), keep the following tips in mind. First, if a police officer says something like "Can I talk with you?" you can say, "I don't have time to talk; I'm in a hurry." (Or something like that; you can also say, "No, I don't want to talk right now.") If the officer persists, ask him "Are you detaining me? Am I free to leave?" If you're free to leave, then leave. If he's detaining you, and persists in asking questions, you have the right to choose not to answer.

Additionally, if an officer asks for permission to search something, just say "no." If he asks you for permission, that means he doesn't have probable cause for a search, so he needs your "consent" in order to do the search. Don't give permission. If he pesters you about why you're refusing a search, you don't have to answer; if you want, you can simply state that you believe in the Constitution.

Finally, if you are arrested, shut up. The police who are questioning you are not interested in helping you out; they are interested in obtaining information in order to prosecute you. During the interrogation, they may deliberately mislead you into thinking that telling them what they want to hear will make things go better for you. (Police interrogation manuals include all sorts of tips about how to trick suspects into confessing.) Just invoke your right to remain silent. Sit quietly in your jail cell, and wait for your attorney. Everything you tell the police in attempt to convince them of your innocence may end up being twisted and used against you. Be quiet, be patient, and wait for your attorney.

30. Honey Catches More Flies than Vinegar

"THOSE WHO HATE YOU CAN'T HARM YOU, UNLESS YOU
HATE THEM BACK, AND THEN YOU DESTROY YOURSELF."
—Richard M. Nixon, farewell speech to White
House staff, August 1974.

Gun control is primarily a moral issue. Like the debate over abortion, the gun control debate is frequently polarizing, because it brings up such visceral questions of fundamental values. Is violent self-defense justified? In a good society, should people always trust the government?

Many folks who have a strong opinion on gun control or abortion issues do so for important personal moral reasons. As a result, some people conclude that people who disagree with them must be immoral people.

The conclusion that people who are wrong about moral issues are immoral themselves is an error made by both sides of the gun control debate. Both our side and the anti-gun side have too often demonized the opposition.

At seminars and debates, Alan and Dave have met many leaders from the anti-gun groups. Almost all of them have been decent, nice persons. Like most of their counterparts in the pro-rights movement, most of the gun control people are making less income than they could working for somebody else (like private industry). They are working on the gun control question because they believe it is important to building a better world.

Father Abraham
The gun prohibition movement, like the pro-slavery movement, was based on the premise that a large number of people were not capable of controlling themselves, and should be guided by their betters. Abraham Lincoln's attitude towards his slaveholding opponents—who perpetrated evils far worse than restricting firearms—provides instruction for our attitude towards our present opponents.

Certainly no person spent more of his life fighting for freedom than Abraham Lincoln. His career as a United States Representative, candidate for Senator, and President of the United States was founded upon the principal that slavery was not simply bad policy, but was fundamentally immoral. As President, he saw hundreds of thousands of innocent young men slaughtered and the United States nearly destroyed in a war that Lincoln thought was brought on by the slave owners. Many Northerners, including the powerful Radical Republican Congressmen, developed a passionate hatred for the South and its leaders.

Lincoln did not. In his second inaugural address, in March 1865, President Lincoln observed that both Confederates and Unionists "read the same Bible and pray to the same God, and each invokes his aid against the other." Although Lincoln thought the slaveholders' claim to have God in their side was wildly wrong, Lincoln acknowledged the frailty of any side's claim to exclusive virtue: "It may seem strange that any men should dare to ask a just God's assistance in wringing their bread from the sweat of other men's faces, but let us judge not that we be judged."

Foreseeing the end of the war, Lincoln called not for punishment of the wicked, but for the nation to move forward "with malice toward, with charity for all."

If the President who led the struggle against slavery could find charity in his heart for slaveholders, it certainly ought to be within our modern reach to find charity for the gun prohibitionists.

Having a humane attitude towards the opposition does not imply any slackening of our own efforts. After all, Lincoln never wavered for a second in his determination to defeat the slave-owners, and to preserve the Union. While holding firm to his own ideals, Lincoln could feel compassion for persons who held opposite ideals.

The Test of Tolerance

In 20th century terms, Lincoln passed what the great theologian Reinhold Niebuhr called "the test of tolerance." The test, wrote Niebuhr in his 1943 book *The Nature and Destiny of Man*, is "not merely to maintain a tolerant attitude towards those who hold beliefs other than our own." Such a simple test would be easy to pass. By falling into "the abyss of skepticism," by denying that there is any absolute goodness or truth, and by pretending that our human actions can have no effect on history, a person could adopt an attitude of passive indifference towards all beliefs.

Such passivity, Niebuhr suggested, was unacceptable. Every person carries a moral obligation to fight for justice and righteousness. "The test of tolerance," Niebuhr continued, "is twofold and includes both the ability to hold vital convictions which lead to action; and also the capacity to preserve the spirit of forgiveness towards those who offend us by holding to convictions which seem untrue to us."

This book is all about the first part of the test: how to take action, to roll up your sleeves to fulfill the vital convictions about freedom that we share.

The second part of the test is also important. If the anti-gun lobby were to achieve its objectives of prohibition on many guns and draconian controls on all the rest, many innocent people— deprived of their right to bear arms—would be raped and murdered by criminals. Our nation would be edging towards a police state; and the repressive measures necessary to enforce gun control would further reduce freedom. Our greatest challenge is to fight against a future which seems so evil— and at the same time not sink into a hatred of the proponents of that future. It is a challenge that must be met not only for ethical reasons, but for practical ones.

As an ethical matter, the world's great religious and philosophical systems stress the necessity of forgiving one's enemies. Persons who hope to receive God's forgiveness must give some of that which they hope to receive.

As a practical matter, failure to pass the test of tolerance diminishes our effectiveness in protecting our rights. Few legislators are gun policy experts, and few have deeply-rooted stands on the issue one way or another. Like all other people, they are often influenced less by what is said, than by how it is said.

Legislators have been alienated, and repressive gun laws enacted in some cities and states because of the hostile attitude of some pro-gun witnesses. When a citizen comes to testify before a city council against gun control, and when he insults the city council, calls gun control advocates Nazis or Communists, and uses his precious minutes of testimony to vent his anger, legislators are often offended and frightened.

The very point of our resistance to paternalistic gun control is that gun owners are responsible, mature people whom their fellow citizens need not fear. The hostile and angry pro-gun witness confirms the fear that some people shouldn't be trusted with deadly weapons.

One Drop of Ink

There's an old saying: "One drop of ink spoils the whole pitcher of milk." The more outrageously hostile and stupid a gun-owner acts, the surer he is to get his picture in the paper or on TV. Throwing a rock through the state capitol window will get you noticed. A lone gun-owner at a rally with a big sign: "Ban 'Liberals', Not Guns" gets a picture of his sign in the paper. Dozens of smaller, more intelligent signs, get ignored by the press.

Sometimes the anti-gun media uses foolish gun nuts to its advantage. The *Los Angeles Times* loves to print letters to the editor from gun owners who are extremist, stupid, paranoid, and prejudiced. People who carry signs or write letters claiming that gun control is a Communist plot are just playing into the hands of the gun grabbers.

But not all the media attention paid to the obnoxious folks on our side is due to bias. As the old saying goes, "You can always get your picture in the paper for pulling your pants down in public." The media has an understandable fixation with people who are extreme or outrageous.

In any case, the message gets out: gun owners are stupid and prejudiced. Gun owners need to learn what more organized activists already know: one bad act at a rally or hearing is likely to get far more press coverage than a multitude of good acts.

Imagine yourself as a person without a strong view on the gun debate. When you listen to caller on a radio talk-show discuss the right to bear arms, or when you read a newspaper letter to the editor on the subject, which person will make you more supportive of the pro-rights side: a hostile person burning with hatred for his enemies? Or a calm person explaining the benefits of the right to bear arms?

In order to win, we must also recognize, as did Father Merrin in *The Exorcist*, that the evil we confront wears many faces, but it is ultimately one and the same. The urge to dominate others against their will comes in various guises. Sometimes it is called gun control; other times, it is called racism, sexism, homophobia, or speciesim.

Anything a gun rights supporter does which reflects bigotry or intolerance harms our cause. Any form of bigotry alienates people unnecessarily. And in the long run, anything that raises the overall supply of hatred in our society helps improve the political climate for people who hate gun owners.

In sociological terms, gun owners are the victims of "moral entrepreneurs," people who specialize in fomenting hatred against other people based on their lifestyles. As victims of moral entrepreneurs, gun owners need to recognize what they have in common with gamblers, drinkers, or sexual minorities. All of them are victims of self-appointed moralists who use the brute force of government to impose their moral beliefs on the rest of the population.

We are never going to win the great gun prohibition war if we have to convince the entire American public that guns are good. We can win by putting our right to do as we wish in the context of the right of all other Americans to do as they wish— even if some of the things that other people do in private are as offensive to us as the private ownership of firearms is to different persons.

As gun rights activists, we have usually exhibited what might sometimes be called male virtues: tenacity, forcefulness and boldness. To this mix, we need to add the ability to listen, empathize, and connect with others on an emotional plane as well as a logical one. In short, we need not just guns, but roses and guns.

The Hate Campaign

If you read the fundraising and promotional literature of the anti-gun organizations, you will find virtually nothing positive inside. The focus of such material is a hate campaign against the National Rifle Association. Josh Sugarmann, one of the leading strategists of the gun prohibition movement, notes with dismay that Handgun Control, Inc. has lost sight of its original goal of saving lives, and instead devotes itself to beating the National Rifle Association.

The hate campaign against the NRA works well enough at raising money, but it also limits the anti-gun lobby. The lobby has very few unpaid volunteers; few of its supporters spend an hour (if that) a year in any kind of volunteer work. Perhaps one reason is that Americans—fortunately—are reluctant to invest their time in an enterprise built so exclusively on negative energy.

In contrast, the pro-rights side attracts thousands of volunteers—people who are motivated by a desire to defend their own positive visions of freedom rather than a hatred of the anti-gun lobby. The pro-gun volunteers bring pleasant memories of plinking with their fathers, honest acceptance of their moral obligation to protect their families, and pride in their nation's tradition of freedom. In the long run, these positive visions generate more success than any hate campaign ever could.

Gun prohibitionists in the 1990s—like slaveholders in the 1860s, American Communists in the 1940s, or segregationists in the 1960s—are a profound threat to freedom. But like slaveholders, Communists, and segregationists, the vast majority are misguided rather than diabolical. Our battle is not with the members or the leaders of these groups, but rather with the principles of tyranny these groups mistakenly support.

Our commitment to protecting Constitutional rights should not depend on whether or not the opponents of rights are nice people. We do not fight for freedom because we derive some joy from attacking freedom's opponents; we fight for freedom because it is right. Just as it is right to fight for freedom, it is right to continue that fight with a spirit of tolerance and forgiveness towards those who disagree with us.

Vicious Tactics

As the saying goes, "Just because you're paranoid doesn't mean they're not out to get you." The "paranoid gun nuts" are correct in their belief that many powerful forces want to take their guns away. The "paranoid" HCI people (and some of their political champions) do, on occasion, sometimes get loony-tunes death threat phone calls from a sick fringe of the gun-owning public.

A James Brady fund-raising letter contains a true story of harassment:

> *a mob of gun nuts organized by the gun lobby disrupted a talk Sarah and I were giving at the University of Nevada by screaming absurd epithets at us such as "Liar!" and "Hitler!" and "Communist!" This is a very disturbing indication of where the NRA's support is based!*

The incident really did happen; it was even reported in *Gun Week*. While insinuating that the NRA organized the demonstration, Mr. Brady doesn't explicitly say so; and, while the NRA wasn't responsible, there is no doubt that the hecklers did shout the Bradys down.

The hecklers did everyone a disservice, and caused particular harm to the grassroots movement for the right to bear arms.

James and Sarah Brady have every First Amendment right to say whatever they want, and the people at the university who came to hear them speak have every First Amendment right to listen.

To "defend" the Second Amendment by squelching the First Amendment betrays the principles that underlie the Bill of Rights.

While the Bradys might, arguably, sometimes be liars, they

are nowhere close to being Nazis or Communists. Just because Communists favor gun control doesn't make all gun controllers Communists. Communists favor heavy taxes, too, but very few proponents of high taxes in the U.S. are Communists.

And even if the Bradys were Nazis or Communists, they would still have the right to speak.

Although the hecklers may have felt happy at being able to release some frustration, they gained our cause no new allies.

Consider the case of someone who was undecided about gun control, and came to hear the Bradys' speech with an open mind. The hecklers' flagrant disrespect for the rights of others might give evidence to the belief that some people really shouldn't be trusted with deadly weapons. In the minds of many uncommitted persons in the audience, the hecklers made a far more effective case for gun control than a Sarah Brady speech ever could.

Before the speech, some anti-Brady protesters had passed out pro-rights fliers as the audience filed in. It's a shame that the hard work of the people who created and distributed the pro-rights fliers may have been negated by hecklers inside.

Simply put, there is no room—absolutely none—for personal intimidation in the gun rights movement. There is no justification for violence, or the threat of violence, against gun control proponents. Late-night phone calls to legislators' homes, verbal abuse of legislative aides, and general immaturity are the tactics of too many gun-owners. These obnoxious tactics are the secret weapon of the anti-gun lobbies.

We always have to remember that what we want is the freedom to own and carry deadly weapons. If you can't use a telephone responsibly, it's awfully difficult to convince a legislator that you and people like you can use a gun responsibly,

The narrow margin of victory for the 1994 prohibition of semiautomatic firearms was created by irresponsible and hate-filled gun activists. If not for the reservoir of bad feelings built up by years of rudeness and incivility on the part of too many gun-owners, Congress would not have voted for the gun prohibition.

If anyone you know engages in any of these reprehensible

tactics, insist that they stop at once, or you will turn them in to the police. And if they don't stop, turn them in. You'll be doing everyone—including the pro-rights movement—a favor.

Cheap Talk

Isn't it amazing how some gun-owners go around claiming that they can't wait for the chance to "blow someone away." Folks who talk like that are doing a disservice to the Second Amendment, and to themselves.

First of all, America isn't Lebanon. If you shoot or kill somebody, no matter how justifiably, you can be sure you're going to have a lot of explaining to do. Put yourselves in the place of a prosecutor or juror trying to decide if your shooting of a burglar was legally necessary. How are they going to react when they find out that for months before the shooting, you were proclaiming your desire to kill someone?

Second, most folks who think it would be fun to kill someone in lawful self-defense have never actually done so. As Lethal Force Institute director Massad Ayoob points out, a great many people who legally and rightfully kill someone still suffer tremendous psychological aftershock. "Only those who've experienced it know how much it takes out of a civilized human being to kill another person, no matter how justifiable the act," Ayoob writes. (*The Truth About Self Protection*, p. 400). To use deadly force to protect yourself or your family from criminal assault may sometimes be a moral duty, but no-one should imagine that the aftermath will be happy.

Finally, cheap talk about the value of human life is tremendously threatening to the 50% of the American population who don't own guns, and to most gun owners as well. The right to bear arms will prosper only as long as most Americans believe that virtually all gun owners are law-abiding, responsible people who can be trusted to own deadly weapons. Any gun owner who claims that he thinks killing is enjoyable is an objective ally of the gun prohibition lobby.

31. The Salami Recipe: Brady II

"THE THINGS I SAW BEGGAR DESCRIPTION. . .THE VISUAL EVI-
DENCE AND THE VERBAL TESTIMONY OF STARVATION, CRUELTY
AND BESTIALITY WERE SO OVERPOWERING. . .I MADE THE VISIT
DELIBERATELY, IN ORDER TO BE IN A POSITION TO GIVE FIRST
HAND EVIDENCE OF THESE THINGS IF EVER, IN THE FUTURE, THERE
DEVELOPS A TENDENCY TO CHARGE THESE ALLEGATIONS TO PRO-
PAGANDA."
—General Dwight David Eisenhower, Ohrdruf concentration
camp, April 15, 1945.

Now that Handgun Control, Inc. has had its way, creating
legislature that requires you to get police permission to buy a
handgun, and outlawing politically incorrect "assault weapons,"
the group is going to give up and leave gun owners alone. Not!
Plenty of gun-owners have kept out of the gun-control
battles so far, in the selfish and foolish belief that the fight didn't
involve them. These gun-owners reasoned that they already had a
handgun, and didn't want to buy an AKS rifle, so the waiting
period and "assault weapon" issues didn't affect them. Well, as a
result of having let Handgun Control, Inc. win on these "minor"
issues, HCI now has a bill with restrictions that will severely in-
fringe the rights of many more gun owners. The HCI bill (known
as "Brady II") is at the top of HCI's agenda.
Here's what Sarah Brady has in store for you next:

"Arsenal" licenses
Any person who owns 20 or more firearms or more than
1,000 rounds of ammunition or primers (i.e. two "bricks" of rimfire
ammo) would be required to get an "arsenal" license.
To obtain a federal arsenal license, you will need to be
fingerprinted, obtain permission of local zoning authorities, and
pay a $300 tax every three years. Your home will be subjected to
unannounced, warrant-less inspection by the government up to
three times a year.

"Arsenal" owners will also have to obtain a $100,000 dollar insurance policy.

If you own less than 20 guns and keep only minimal ammunition supplies on hand, don't think that you're exempt from the "arsenal" license. "Brady II" redefines "firearm" to include magazines and "any part of the action" (such as pins, springs, or screws).

In other words, if you have two Colt pistols, three Remington rifles, and four magazines (of any size) for each gun, then you own an "arsenal." Or if you own two guns, six magazines, and a box of disassembled gun parts that contains five springs, five pins, and five screws, then you own 23 firearms and must obtain an "arsenal" license.

Licenses

As for folks who don't own "arsenals," HCI still has plenty for them.

Every handgun buyer will be required to obtain a state handgun license. The license will be good for no more than two years. No-one will be able to obtain a license without passing a state-controlled "safety" course. The fees for the license and the safety course will have no limits. The fees might easily be set far in excess of the state cost of providing the license and the course; instead, the fees will be a source of general revenue.

Nothing will prevent licensing authorities from taking nearly a year to issue a license (the current practice in New York City), and nothing will prevent the authorities from making the "safety" test so rigorous that almost no-one except a Class A IPSC shooter could pass.

By the way, the fact that you have been shooting handguns for 50 years, or are an NRA certified safety instructor, or are a competitive target shooter will not exempt you from the requirement to pay for the government "safety" class.

Every handgun transfer (including your father-in-law giving you his old revolver) will be subject to these restrictions. In addition, every handgun transferred will have to be registered by make and serial number.

Punitive Taxes

Currently, the price of guns and ammunition is increased by an 11% federal excise tax, revenues from which go to improve hunting habitat and fund the development of target ranges. HCI's "Brady II" would increase the taxes to 30% on handguns and 50% on ammunition. So a $300 pistol would cost $390, and a $10 box of ammunition would cost $15.

The tax revenues, instead of being spent on shooting sports, would be spent on health care. Should if law-abiding target shooters should be held responsible for picking up the tab for current and future federal socialized medicine boondoggles?

It will become a federal crime to buy more than one hand-gun a month. Too bad if you see a nice pair of old West revolvers you'd like to buy at a gun show.

The first "Brady Bill" was enacted by Congress because HCI promised to adopt the NRA's "instant check" idea. No later than 1998, the Brady bill's handgun waiting period will expire. It will be replaced by an "instant check" on the retail sale of all firearms.

"Brady II" renounces the compromise that made enactment of Brady I possible. A permanent 7-day waiting period will be imposed on all handgun transfers (including gifts between family members).

The list of persons banned by law from owning any gun will be expanded. If you got into a bar fight 20 years ago, and pleaded guilty to misdemeanor third-degree assault, you will be barred for the rest of your life from owning any gun. (And subject to a mandatory five years in federal prison if you were caught.) Any other crime, no matter how petty, involving the use or threatened use of force will likewise merit lifetime prohibition from owning a gun.

Suppose that during an acrimonious divorce 15 years ago, you and your ex-wife both obtained a restraining order, simply ordering each of you to stay away from each other. A restraining order would also become a permanent bar to gun possession.

Possession of handguns or handgun ammunition by a person under the age of 21, or possession of any guns or ammunition by a person under the age of 16, will be illegal. So forget about giving your 15 year old nephew a .22 rifle as a gift.

All firearms will have to be "properly stored" to prevent access by anyone under the age of 16. If a 15 year old burglar broke into your home, stole a gun, and shot a fellow gang member with it, you would be guilty of a crime and could be sued by the gang member.

Seven-round magazines

All magazines which hold more than 6 rounds of ammunition would be outlawed. Possession of existing magazines with a larger capacity would be allowed under the same terms as are now applicable to possession of machine guns: a 10-point FBI fingerprint; an expensive federal tax; and possession only allowed if a letter of authorization from the local police chief is obtained.

Gun shows would be destroyed, since licensed firearms dealers would not be allowed to sell guns at the show.

Small handguns

There are plenty more provisions in Brady II, the worst of which is a ban on so-called "Saturday Night Specials." A "Saturday Night Special" will be defined as:

1. A handgun with any parts made of zinc alloy.
2. Any handgun that uses .22 short ammunition (or course many guns that use .22 LR can also use .22 short).
3. Any revolver with a barrel less than 3 inches.
4. Any pistol with combined height and length of less than 10 inches.
5. Any pistol without a "positive manually operated safety device."

Do you suppose that if HCI passes "Brady II" that there won't be a "Brady III," and a "Brady IV"? And what will be in "Brady III" and "Brady IV"? Mrs. Brady has already told us:

She wants a "needs-based licensing" system, under which

no one could own any gun unless the local police chief decided that the person "needed" to have the gun. ("A Little Gun Control, a Lot of Guns," *New York Times*, Aug. 15, 1993, p. B1).

Ownership of a gun for protection would not be considered a legitimate "need." Says Mrs. Brady, "To me, the only reason for guns in civilian hands is for sporting purposes." (Tom Jackson, "Keeping the Battle Alive," *Tampa Tribune*, Oct. 21, 1993.)

32. *The British Lesson*

"IN GERMANY, THEY FIRST CAME FOR THE COMMUNISTS, AND I DIDN'T SPEAK UP BECAUSE I WASN'T A COMMUNIST. THEN, THEY CAME FOR THE JEWS, AND I DIDN'T SPEAK UP BECAUSE I WASN'T A JEW...THEN THEY CAME FOR THE CATHOLICS. I DIDN'T SPEAK UP BECAUSE I WAS A PROTESTANT. THEN THEY CAME FOR ME, AND THERE WAS NO ONE LEFT TO SPEAK UP."
—Reverend Martin Niemoller, German Lutheran pastor arrested by the Gestapo in 1937.

Do the anti-gun lobbies want to take away everybody's hunting rifles? Not at all. As a result, some sportsmen find nothing objectionable in the lobbies' calls for "moderate" gun control. However, the fact that the lobbies really, sincerely, don't want to take everyone's guns away does not reduce the danger that the lobbies pose to the ownership of guns.

In Britain, a century of severe gun control has nearly obliterated the ranks of gun owners. Yet, while gun crime is very low in Britain (and was even lower before the gun controls were enacted), occasional gun crimes furnish the pretext for an outcry for the abolition of all guns. Britain began this century with widespread civilian gun ownership, no gun controls, and virtually no gun crime. Britain will end the century with the tiny ranks of gun owners just a step away from full prohibition.

The British gun owners got themselves in their predicament by accepting more and more "moderate" proposals for control. The sum of these "moderate" proposals made gun ownership difficult for most people, and has left the remaining gun owners with too small a mass to be a strong political force. Will American gun owners follow the same road to self-destruction in coming decades by accepting the first "moderate" proposals of the gun prohibition lobbies?

33. *No Apologies for the Constitution*

". . . WE WROTE A FAIRLY RADICAL CONSTITUTION WITH A
RADICAL BILL OF RIGHTS, GIVING A RADICAL AMOUNT OF
INDIVIDUAL RESPONSIBILITY TO AMERICANS. . .
        WHAT'S HAPPENED IN AMERICA TODAY IS. . .A LOT OF
PEOPLE SAY THERE'S TOO MUCH PERSONAL FREEDOM. WHEN
PERSONAL FREEDOM'S BEING ABUSED, YOU HAVE TO MOVE TO
LIMIT IT."
—President Clinton, bragging about plans for gun sweeps in
                public housing projects, MTV, April 19, 1994.

Some folks think that all of our Constitutional freedoms
are an unalloyed benefit. Don't believe them. Most of the freedoms in the Bill of Rights exact a heavy price from society. That's
why most other countries, including all of our democratic allies,
don't protect these freedoms with anything near the stringency
we do.

Take the Fourth Amendment which prohibits unreasonable searches and seizures. Many other democracies have a similar rule, but none of them have what our Supreme Court invented:
the exclusionary rule. Under the exclusionary rule, if police seize
evidence illegally, the evidence can't be admitted into court no
matter how important the evidence is.

Foreign visitors are shocked when they find out about the
exclusionary rule. Over the years the exclusionary rule has freed
thousands of hardened criminals who have laughed at a society
that let them go free. No doubt these thousands of freed criminals
went on to commit tens of thousands more crimes.

Most democratic countries forbid physical torture of a
criminal suspect, but only in America are the police hindered with
an elaborate set of rules that are designed to prevent psychologi-
cally coercing a suspect.

The hard truth is that without some pressure from the
police, most criminals won't confess. In many cases there isn't
enough tangible evidence to convict someone without a confes-

sion. This is why the British allow a suspect to be held without outside contact for several days. The Japanese allow a person to be secretly detained for weeks at a time. In America, however, suspects must be told that they are allowed a free lawyer, to whom they have almost immediate access.

Criminal procedure isn't the only Constitutional field that features strict rules. Take the First Amendment. Current libel laws make it almost impossible for any public figure to recover damages for even the most vicious lies. The victim of libel must prove that the author misstated the facts "knowingly or recklessly." Since it's pretty hard to get inside someone's head and prove what he was thinking, the vast majority of libel plaintiffs lose.

Losing your reputation to a libel is horrible, but it's nothing like losing your son or your daughter to some "cult" leader. In a large part of the rest of the world, Jim Jones would have been thrown into an insane asylum or prison long before he led his victims off to poison death in Guyana.

Many people believe that no Constitutional provision causes more damage than the Second Amendment's right to keep and bear arms. These people concede that all-out national gun control will not keep professional criminals from buying guns, but they believe that controls would make it harder for young hoods to acquire the tools for a spur of the moment mugging.

In addition, a widespread ban on gun ownership, if successful, theoretically would prevent many gun accidents.

Are strict Constitutional freedoms are a bad idea? Not at all. By refusing to sanction illegal police behavior, a strong exclusionary rule protests the integrity of the judicial system. Unless illegally seized evidence is kept out of the courtroom, there is no practical incentive for the police to obey rules about searches and seizures.

Tough rules about coerced confessions were created precisely because lesser rules proved insufficient. In countries like Japan and Britain, where suspects can be held without outside contact, police abuse and torture of innocent suspects can and does occur.

America's broad freedom of religion does allow "cults" to flourish, but one person's cult is another person's true revelation. America is the birthplace of Baptists, Christian Scientists, Unitarians, Latter Day Saints, Reform Jews and many other groups that have blossomed under the bright sun of America's religious freedom. These groups are considered "cults" in many other nations, but America's tolerant spirit recognizes that there are many paths to God, and that any attempt by the government to direct religious belief will ultimately harm both religion and society.

America's high standards of freedom of the press have made the American press especially bold about ferreting out wrong-doing in high places. Unafraid of being slapped with a libel lawsuit, American reporters were able to uncover corrupt affairs such as Watergate and the Iran-Contra scandal, affairs that would have remained secret in other countries.

The Second Amendment's right to bear arms inflicts (if the gun control lobbyists are right) significant costs on society. Part of the pro-rights response to the gun ban movement has been to point out that gun control does nothing to reduce harm associated with guns. Gun rights advocates also point out that firearms are used to prevent violent felonies hundreds of thousands of times a year. True enough, but it is also important to look at the long-run picture.

Whether or not widespread gun ownership increases or decreases accidents or crime, gun ownership is a long-term "holocaust insurance policy." Because the American people are armed, no American government could successfully perpetrate a policy of mass murder. In every country where genocide has occurred—including Cambodia, Uganda, the Soviet Union, and Nazi Germany—the perpetrators have first disarmed their future victims. The ability of the American people to forcefully resist a tyrannical government could, in the long run, prevent tens of millions of deaths.

Looking at the big picture, the risks of a single maniac with a gun he bought over the counter are outweighed by the risks of a maniac with a standing army and no forceful citizen opposition. Hitler and Tojo killed far more people in a few years than all the world's private gun misusers since the invention of gunpowder. Hitler and Tojo were able to enjoy their monopoly of power in part because they had disarmed all potential resistance. Hitler's gun policies, like those proposed by many American gun control advocates, limited gun possession only to people who had been approved by the government, and allowed only the possession of guns which were deemed suitable for sports by the government. (For more on German gun controls and genocide, see *Lethal Laws*, discussed in chapter 13.)

The same points made about the Second Amendment apply to the rest of the Bill of Rights. Yes, press abuses of free speech cause harm every day of the year. But in the long run, much more serious harms could be inflicted by a government that had the ability to control the press. Criminals who are set free because of Bill of Rights protections cause harm, but a government that can search people without regard for privacy rights, or throw people in a police station without telling their relatives, can cause greater harm.

One of the important reasons that the American Bill of Rights was created was that its authors knew that there would always be short-run pressures for more government power in order to deal with the social dislocations that sometimes result from liberty. The founders knew that certain freedoms, including free speech and the right to keep and bear arms, should be placed beyond the reach of transient and excitable majorities. In the long run, enforcing firm restraints on government is the most important way to protect public safety.

34. The Price of Freedom

"It was two by the village clock,
when he came to the bridge in Concord town.
He heard the bleating of the flock,
and the twitter of birds among the trees,
and felt the breath of the morning breeze
blowing over the meadow brown.
And one was safe and asleep in his bed
who at that bridge would be the first to fall,
who that day would be lying dead,
pierced by the British musket ball.

You know the rest. In the books you have read
how the British regulars fired and fled,
how the farmers gave them ball for ball,
from behind each fence and farmyard wall,
chasing the redcoats down the land,
then crossing the fields to emerge again
under the trees at the turn of the road,
and only pausing to fire and load."

—Henry Wadsworth Longfellow, "The Midnight Ride
of Paul Revere"

What happened to those 57 men who signed the Declaration of Independence? Five were captured, tortured, and executed by the British as traitors. Nine were killed in battle, or died from wounds caused by battle. The homes of twelve were destroyed. Others had children who were killed in battle or captured by the British.

Almost all of the signers were men of learning and accomplishment. Had they stayed out of the conflict with the British, their lives and property would have remained secure. But these men knew that their sacred Honor would be forever lost if they failed to stand for freedom in its moment of peril.

Fame was a reward for only a few of the signers. Most of

them are obscure to us today. Virginia merchant Carter Braxton had his property destroyed by the British, and died penniless.

British troops kidnapped the wife of Francis Lewis while he was away from home. The Redcoats stole everything they could, and burned the rest to the ground. Mrs. Lewis was held prisoner in a filthy, unheated room without even a bed. After several months in captivity, she died.

John Hart was forced to flee his dying wife's bedside. Evading the British, he lived in caves and forests for over a year. When he returned, he found his wife dead, his 13 children missing without a trace, and his farm destroyed. He died a few weeks later.

These men gave all they had for a conflict that began when the British tried to seize an American cannon in Lexington, Massachusetts and American gunpowder in Williamsburg, Virginia.

At Gettysburg, at Normandy, and at thousands more obscure places, Americans laid down their lives to preserve that legacy of freedom and to defeat evil governments that believed in enslaving and disarming "inferior" people.

What legacy will you help leave to the following generations of Americans? In a period when the struggle for freedom is comparatively easy, will our legacy be a full and vigorous Bill of Rights? Or will this generation, through inaction, stand aside without protest as our freedoms are eroded and the struggle of future generations is made all the more difficult?

35. *Never Surrender*

"Danger and deliverance make their advances together;
and it is only in the last push that one or the other takes
the lead."
—Thomas Paine, *The American Crisis*, Dec. 23, 1776.

Be patient with yourself, and with the pace of progress. Be patient with yourself because you, as a fallible human being, will inevitably make mistakes. (If you're infallible and superhuman, please contact Alan right away; he'd like to make you a job offer.) Be patient with other people; they're even more fallible than you.

The battle to protect the right to bear arms will not be won with finality tomorrow, or next year, or perhaps even next century. Many of your projects will not lead to spectacular results, but to results that you can't even see, to small, but significant changes in how other people view the pro-rights cause. Be assured, however, that you will be doing good, and that even if you can't see your results, posterity will.

We live in a privileged age and place. You don't have to risk your life leading a guerrilla raid on the Redcoats. You don't have to face Nazi or Communist soldiers. Unless you're a cop, you probably don't face the risk of being harassed at work for speaking out on your own time.

Like the American militiamen who fought the War for Independence, our side fights an opponent with tremendous resources. We lack their near-total control of the national media, their access to the Hollywood propaganda machine. Likewise, during the War for Independence, the British Navy controlled the coast, the British Army occupied nearly every major city, the British Generals were the best in the world, the British Empire was the largest empire in history, and the British Redcoats and their Hessian mercenaries were better trained and better armed than the American "rabble" that opposed them.

But that American "rabble"—which included a large shares

of "gun nuts"—had resources that the British Empire could not match. In every county in America were men who were ready to carry on guerrilla warfare, not matter how badly outnumbered they were. Trained not to submissive obedience but to independence and action, the American militiamen devised one tactic after another to outwit the rigid British commanders. Most importantly, the American militiamen never gave up, because they knew that freedom for themselves, their children, and the world would prosper or perish based on what they did. After many defeats, and many years of struggle, the American militia triumphed.

Today the weapon of freedom is, providentially, the pen and not the sword. Persons who support freedom need not meet in secret. But our struggle remains the same as it ever was: the eternal contest between freedom and repression, between individual rights and coercive government.

Our ancestors in this struggle are not only those who took up arms in defense of freedom, but also those who took up the pen and the soapbox: the giants like pamphleteer Tom Paine, abolitionist Frederick Douglas, and civil rights attorney Clarence Darrow.

When you join the struggle to defend our Constitution, you join the ranks of these heroes. Be proud of the American tradition of responsible gun ownership. Be proud of the American tradition of standing up for individual rights.

You are a freedom fighter.

QUANTITY DISCOUNTS
MORE Things You Can Do To Defend Your Gun Rights
Give a copy to everyone you know!

Now is the time to get this book into the hands of every American. Order 25, 50, or 100 copies. Send them to your friends. Give them to business associates. Mail one to everyone you know.

DISCOUNT SCHEDULE

1 copy	$9.95	25 copies	$175.00
5 copies	$45.00	50 copies	$300.00
10 copies	$85.00	100 copies	$500.00
	500 copies	$2,000.00	

ORDER YOURS TODAY!
Call (206) 454-7009 or use the coupon below

Merril Press
P.O. Box 1682
Bellevue, WA 98009

Please send me _____ copies of **MORE Things You Can Do To Defend Your Gun Rights**. Enclosed is a check or money order in the amount of $_____.
Please charge my: ☐ VISA   ☐ MasterCard
Signature_____
Print Name_____
Street_____
City_____
State_____ZIP_____
Phone (_____)_____